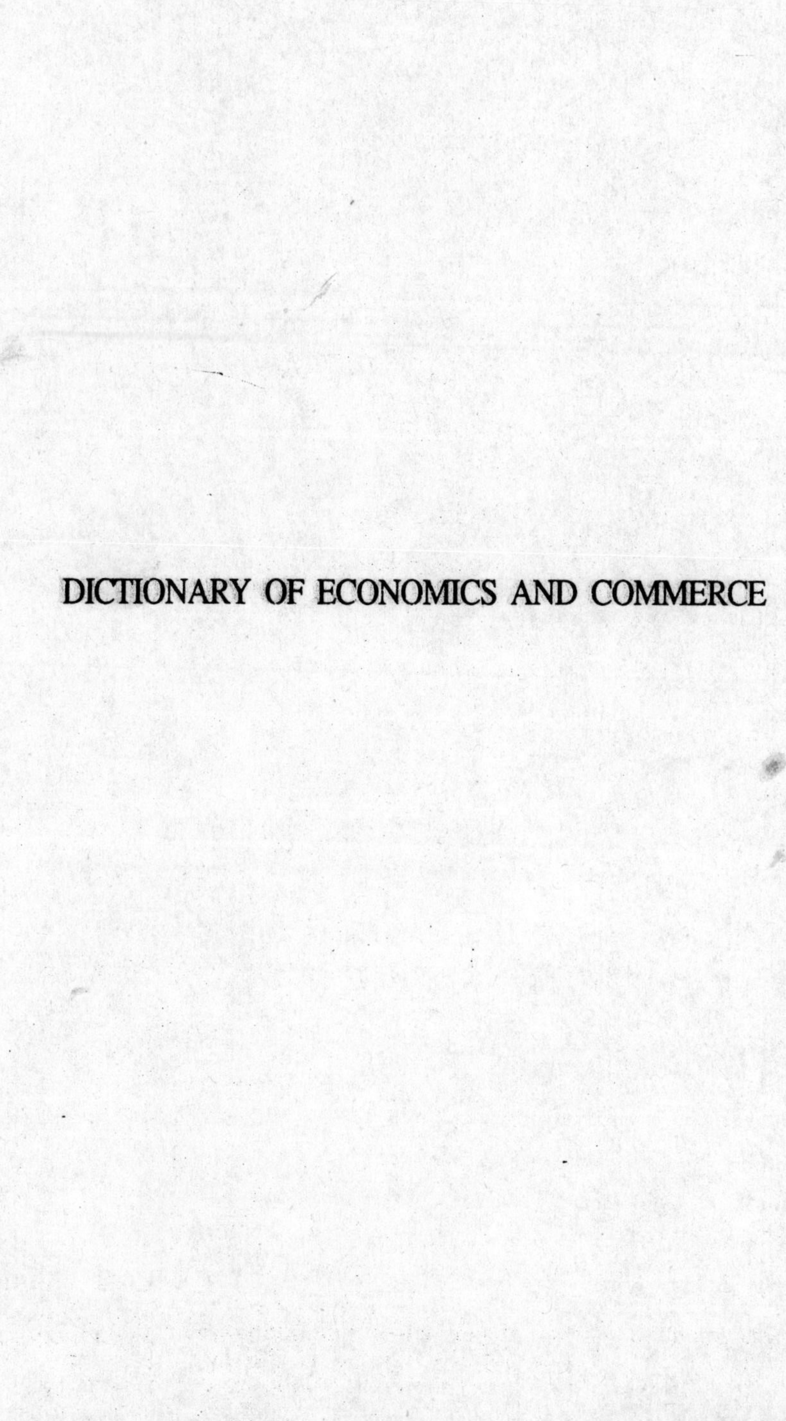

DICTIONARY OF ECONOMICS AND COMMERCE

DICTIONARY OF ECONOMICS AND COMMERCE

G.C. Pande
R. Chopra

ANMOL PUBLICATIONS PVT LTD
New Delhi-110 002

ANMOL PUBLICATIONS PVT LTD
4374/4B, Ansari Road, Daryaganj
New Delhi-110 002

Dictionary of Economics and Commerce

First Edition 1990
Reprint 1991
Reprint 1992
Reprint 1993
Reprint 1994
Reprint 1995
Second Revised Edition 1996
Reprint, 2002

PRINTED IN INDIA

Published by J.L. Kumar for Anmol Publications Pvt Ltd, New Delhi-110 002 and Printed at Mehra Offset Press, Delhi.

Preface

This dictionary has been revised to include the most frequently used terms from the various fields of economics and commerce. An attempt has been carefully made to edit the entries in a clear and lucid style to provide both straight forward definitions and invaluable background information. Some terms are explained quite briefly, others at some length. This dictionary may act as a handy and reliable source for definitions, statements, commercial laws, theories and principles of both economics and commerce.

When a dictionary of this kind is being compiled, it becomes essential to consult the standard works and seek the advice of colleagues to all of whom the editors are deeply indebted.

This dictionary will be of immense value to undergraduate and postgraduate students and to those appearing for competitive examinations, research scholars, teachers and authors but also to economists, businessmen, tax-payers, investors and insurance agents, economic administrators, planners, journalists, business managers and the general reader with a little bid of interest in economics and commerce.

Finally, the editors express their sincere thanks to the publishers and printer for printing this book promptly.

All comments from users on omissions or shortcomings will be highly appreciated.

G.C. Pande
R. Chopra

A

Abandoned Option. A share option not exercised because the price is against the buyer (or taker) on declaration day, i.e. the situation has unprofitable.

Abatement. (1) Extinguishing all or part of a claim. A tax abatement is really a cancellation of the tax claim.

(2) Legal steps to terminate a nuisance.

Abatement Cost. The cost of abating a nuisance like pollution or congestion.

ABC Analysis. In stock control, this term refers to a process whereby components, sub-assemblies and other items are classified, generally by annual usage and value. By multiplying the price and annual usage, the value of each item of stock held and the frequency with which it is used can be calculated, yielding the stock controller some idea of the costs of holding stocks and information to help in rationalizing inventory levels. Typically, such an analysis shows that around 20 per cent of items account for 80 per cent of usage or value and these are called 'A' items; similarly, 'B' items (around 25 per cent) account for the next 15 per cent and the remainder is made up of 'C' items.

Ability to Pay Tax Theory. The most common principle on which the tax burden is based. Income, property, or consumption can be used as a basis for measuring ability to pay. Theoretically ability to pay is measured by sacrifice (loss of utility).

Abnormal Performance Index. An index of non-systematic changes in share prices which is used to study the effects of unexpected changes in accounting earnings.

Abnormal Spoilage. The spoilage which should not arise under efficient operations.

Above the Line. That part of the profit and loss account (income statement) above the measure of earnings on which Earnings Per Share (EPS) is based.

Absenteeism. The failure to report for work although the terms of the labour contract need the worker to do so and the contract has been still operational.

Absenteeism Rate. The number of days of lost time in relation to the number of possible working days is referred to as the absenteeism rate. The most frequently used formula is A = L/F, where A = absenteeism rate, L = number of days of lost time, and F = number of possible working days.

Absolute Income Hypothesis. According to this hypothesis, consumption expenditures (C) have been a function solely of current personal disposable income (Y_d): $C = C(Y_d)$. This view of the determinants of consumption was discussed in the general theory by Keynes.

Absolute Monopoly. The control of the entire output of a commodity or service, for which there exists no substitute, by a single producer or supplier.

Absorption Costing. Refers to a method of costing in which both variable and fixed overhead have been treated as Product Costs and, to the extent that goods manufactured during the period remain unsold, carried forward as part of the cost of stocks (inventories).

Abstinence. Refers to, the sacrifice of current consumption to increase future consumption usually be enabling resources to get directed to the production of capital goods.

Abstinence or Agio Theory of Interest. A theory which states that interest is a payment for abstaining from current consumption. This is but a partial explanation as there have been other reasons for saving.

Accelerated Depreciation. Depreciation at a faster rate than usual. In recent years used to refer to tax amortization certificates which upon government consent allow writing off an asset in five years for income tax purposes regardless of its life.

Accelerating Inflation. Means increasingly sharp rise in the rate of inflation.

Acceleration Clause. The term used for a provision in an agreement for the repayment of a loan by instalments that if a specified number of instalments are not paid then all the outstanding payments would become due immediately.

Accelerator Principle. The theory which states that the level of aggregate net investment has been found to depend on the expected change in output. In its native form it can be put as follows:

$$I_t = a\,\Delta Y_{f-1} + b$$

where 'a' denotes the accelerator coefficient, 'Δ' means 'small change in', and ΔY_{t-1}' implies the change in the level of output in the previous year. ΔY_{t-1} thus becomes a proxy for the expected change in output, and b is replacement investment.

Acceptance. The agreement of a party to a contract or other arrangement submitted to him for consideration.

Acceptance Bank. An organisation that specialises in accepting or guaranteeing domestic and foreign bills of exchange.

Acceptance Credit. Also termed as a 'letter of acceptance'. It is a method of payment which is widely used in inland and international trade. If the credit of a foreign import merchant is regarded satisfactory an accepting house may open an acceptance credit for him in a bank. A purchase from an exporter may then be financed by means of a bill of exchange drawn on the accepting house. The exporter can then obtain his money quickly as the bill can be easily discounted in the bank.

Acceptance Houses. The specialised firms which act as agent between the importers and exporters. Acceptance Houses handle the international transactions and accept the bills of exchange drawn on the merchants unknown. Accepting Houses charge a commission for the acceptance of guarantee of bills.

Acceptance Sampling. In an audit context, a sampling plan which in designed to control the levels of both Alpha and Beta Risk.

Accident Insurance. A contract for payment of a certain sum in the event of injury or death by accident. In the case of injury, payment of a certain sum per week for a limited number of weeks is made, usually including medical expenses. Usually classed as a special type of life insurance.

Accepting House. A financial institution which has been accepting bills of exchange, with such backing the bills command a higher price.

Accessions Tax. In many countries, it is a tax which is levied on gifts and inherited property.

Accommodating Credit. A term which is frequently used for referring to the 'automatic financing' of deficits, e.g. when an exporter provides credit to the importer.

Accommodating Movements. Transfers of gold and convertible currency abroad to over-come deficits in the total balance of payment of a country.

Accommodation Bill. A bill which is drawn, accepted or endorsed for the sole purpose of discounting it, no goods being given or received for it, thus offering short-term cash accommodation.

Account. Refers to a running record of transactions which is taking place between two transactors, who may be two departments of one business, and a basic element in all systems of recording business transactions.

Accountability. The obligation of stewards or agents to provide relevant and reliable information relating to resources over which they have control and which have effects on other (principals).

Accountancy. Often used merely as a synonym for Accounting, but some writers distinguish between accounting and the Profession of accountancy.

Accountant. A person who is qualified in book-keeping and allied subjects.

Account Current. Refers to a statement in debit and credit form setting out in chronological order the transactions that have taken place between two persons or organizations. Interest is sometimes calculated at agreed rates on the balances outstanding from time to time.

Account Day. Refers to the day on which all deals for a stock exchange Account are settled.

Accounting. The term used for the preparation and communication to users of financial and economic information. The information ideally have certain Qualitative Characteristics.

Accounting Bases. The term used for accounting standards, methods which have been developed for applying fundamental accounting concepts to financial transactions and to items in financial statements.

Accounting History. Refers to the study of the evolution of accounting thought, practices and institutions in response to changes in the environment and the needs of society, and of the effect of this evolution on the environment.

Accounting Costs. Costs regarded as recorded costs only; economic costs might be larger or smaller when alternative costs or opportunity costs and external effects have been taken into account.

Accounting Identity (or Equation). Refers to the relationship which holds among Assets, Liabilities and Capital, i.e., assets equals liabilities plus capital or assets minus liabilities equals capital.

Accounting Journals. Journals which are aimed at professional or academic accountants or both.

Accounting Machine. A machine which is designed for the operation of a particular accounting function such as, for example, sales ledger accounting.

Accounting Period. The period between two successive balance sheets and that for which profit and loss accounts (income statements) and funds statements are prepared.

Accounting Principles. In company law the principles according to which the amounts of all items in a company's accounts are to be determined.

Accounting Rate of Return. A method of capital investment Appraisal which measures the average net profit of a project as a percentage of the average book value.

Accounting Records. Ledgers, Journals and supporting documents. Every company is required by law to keep accounting records sufficient to show and explain the company's transactions.

Accounting Reference Period. A Company's accounting period as notified to the Registrar of Companies.

Accounting Standards. Accounting rules and procedures which are related to measurement, valuation and disclosure prepared by such bodies as the Accounting Standards Committee (ASC).

Accounting System. A set of records and procedures which are designed so as to handle in routine fashion the transactions (especially those concerning cash, sales and purchases) and other events affecting an enterprise's operations, performance and financial position.

Accounts. In general, all the Accounting Records of an enterprise.

Account Sales. A document which shows the gross and net proceeds of a consignment of goods sold by one person for the account and risk of another, and giving details of the expenses and charges in connection with the sale.

Accounts Payable. Amounts which are owing by an enterprise, distinguished from Accrued Expenses and other Current Liabilities not arising out of trading transactions.

Accounts Receivable. Amounts which are owing to an enterprise, distinguished from Prepaid Expenses and other Current Assets not arising out of trading transactions.

Accrual Accounting. An accounting system which, unlike Cash

Flow Accounting, recognizes revenues and expenses as they are earned or incurred, not as cash is received or paid.

Accured Expenses. The expenses (e.g. wages) which have been incurred but not yet paid at balance sheet date.

Accumulated Depreciation. The cumulative amount of Depreciation which is written off a Fixed Asset as at a balance sheet date.

Acquisition Accounting. The preparation of Consolidated Financial Statements on the assumption that one company has acquired another rather than merged with another.

Active Balance. In monetary theory, there are some models which postulate a division of the money supply into active balances, which are money stocks that turn over actively within periods determined by the intervals between payments; and idle balances, which are money stocks not used in the circuit of regular payments.

Active Circulation. That part of the note issue of the Reserve Bank in circulation at any given time.

Activists. The descriptive of economists who believe in the use of monetary and fiscal policies for controlling the economy, and who tend to recognise and favour a large role for government in the economy. In particular, activists believe in the possibility of successful fine-tuning.

Acts of Bankruptcy. Refers to the statutory tests of Insolvency.

Actual Cost. The cost which is determined on the basis of historical costs incurred as distinct from budgeted or standard costs.

Additional Worker Hypothesis. On this argument, the fall in family labour force in the hope of finding a job so as to maintain family income.

Address Principle. In a planned economy such as the USSR each target possesses an organization or 'address' which has been responsible for carrying it out.

Adjusting Entries. Refers to the entries which are made at balance sheet date in an Accrual Accounting system in order to take account of such items as depreciation, closing stock (if a Perpetual Inventory is not in operation), prepaid expenses, accrued expenses, provisions for doubtful debts and accrued interest receivable.

Adjustment Process. The adjustment mechanisms which operate in the international economy for removing imbalances in foreign payments.

Ad Valorem: (according to the value). This kind of levey is generally made on items like stamp duties, excise, customs etc.

Ad Valorem Tax. A duty which has been imposed on commodities in proportion to their value, i.e. a duty which a expressed as a percentage and not a flat amount. It has been commonly used in respect of import tariffs.

Advance Corporation Tax (ACT). Under the imputation system of corporation tax, the tax payable in advance when a company pays a dividend.

Advancement. A payment by a parent, during his or her lifetime, to a child of what the child would receive, as heir or beneficiary, at the death of the parent.

Advanced Countries. The dividing line between advanced countries and developing countries has been known from per capita income.

Age Earnings Profile. The relationship between earnings and age. The simplest age earnings profile is expected to be a horizontal line which is stepping up from zero at the age of leaving school with the size of step being determined by the quantity of schooling.

Agglomeration Economies. Cost savings in an economic activity which arise from enterprises or activities locating near one another.

Aggregate Demand Curve. Means the schedule which details the quantity of net national product that would be purchased at each general price level.

Aggregate Demand Function. A relationship between the planned level of real spending or demand for goods and the level of prices, given the quantity of money and fiscal policy; the function gives an equilibrium relationship between aggregate spending and the price level.

Aggregate Supply. Means the total supply of goods and services in an economy which is available to meet aggregate demand. The stream of goods and services comprises domestic production together with imports.

Aggregate Supply Curve. Refers to the schedule which is detailing the quantity of net national product that would be supplied at each general price level given constant price expectations.

Aggregation. Refers to the bringing together or summing of primary data. For example, the national income has been an aggregate, in contrast with the income of an individual.

Aggregative Index. The term used for an index number which has been constructed by aggregating a number of items, e.g., Laspeyers' Index and Paasche's Index.

Aggregate Model. Refers to an econometric model in which the variables have been themselves constructed from groups of individual variables, as when a price index number gets substituted for a set of prices.

Agio. Means a charge for changing one currency into another, or for changing paper money into coin; the excess value of one currency over another at the prevailing official rate of exchange.

Agio Theory of Interest. An explanation of interest as the result of postponement of present consumption to future consumption and the payment of an agio (premium) for the postponement.

Agriculture Bank. A bank which is especially established to assist the agricultural development by providing loans to a larger duration.

Aid India Consortium. A group of countries of Western Europe and North America that extend aid to India collectively. The individual member contributions are also announced.

Allocation Function. Refers to that part of government tax and expenditure policy which deals with influencing the provision of goods and services in the economy.

Allocation Problem. Refers to the problem of how to allocate cost of services purchased, when only part of the services have been used up in one accounting period. The allocation is between costs to be charged against the revenue of the period and costs accured as an asset to be used in future periods.

Allotment. The term used for the allocation of shares by the directors of a company following applications for them by intending shareholders.

Alpha Risk and Beta Risk. In an audit sampling context, the risks that an auditor will reject a population when he should have accepted it (alpha risk) and that an auditor will accept a population when he should have rejected it (beta risk).

Amalgamation. Refers to the absorption by one company of the business and net assets of another company, the latter company being dissolved or both companies being dissolved and a new company formed to take over both business.

Amortization. Refers to the redemption of a loan by means of payments into a Sinking Fund.

Amortization Payment. Provision for repayment of debt by means of accumulating a sinking fund, through regular payment, which may be used to settle debt in instalments or in lump sum.

Annual Equivalent Cost. Refers to a variant of the Net Present Value (NPV) method of Capital Investment Appraisal. The NPV is converted into an annual equivalent cost in which the NPVs have been divided by the annuity factor.

Annual Financial Statement. Refers to an annual estimate of all anticipated revenue and expenditure.

Annual General Meeting (AGM). The annual general meeting of an organization and in particular a meeting of the members (i.e. the shareholders) of a company held at intervals of not more than fifteen months.

Annual Report. Any report prepared at yearly intervals and in particular the report required by law or other regulation to be made annually by the directors of a company to its shareholders.

Annual Return. In the UK, a document which must be completed by a company within a fixed period of the Annual General Meeting and forwarded forthwith to the Registrar of Companies.

Analysis of Variance. (Also known as ANOVA). Refers to the breakdown of the total variation in a dependent variable (with total variation defined as the sum of squared deviations from its mean) into the proportions which have been accounted for by variation in individual, or groups of explanatory variables, and the unexplained or residual variation.

Anarchy. Refers to the theory which states that social and economic affairs of individuals ought not to be restricted by any government interference. It is a more extreme view than that of laissez-faire or liberalism.

Annuity. A fixed amount of money to be paid to a person every year. It may be either because of some liability or as a result of a settlement; Payment will continue for difinite period.

Application Money. The amount per share or unit of stock payable on application for a new issue of shares or debentures.

Applied Economics. Branch of economic science which is devoted to the study of practical problems, utilising the principles and tools of economic analysis offered by theoretical economics.

Appraiser. A professional valuer of property.

Appreciation. The increase in value of certain assets. Some assets like land, building etc. become more valuable as time passes, i.e., they appreciate in value. The opposite phenomenon of depreciation.

Appropriation Account. An account which is prepared at the end of the financial year of the spending by central government departments of monies voted by Parliament.

A Priori. Relates to speculation or reasoning which has been prior to actual experience. As reasoning it proceeds deductively from cause to effect; such speculation or reasoning stands in contrast to an appeal in evidence. The term is often used as a synonym for 'on theoretical grounds'.

A Priori Theories of Accounting. Refers to the development and rationalization of systems of accounting valuation and measurement by means of deductive reasoning. A priori theories proceed from cause to effect making use of assumed axioms rather than of experience.

Arbitrage. Refers to the simultaneous purchases of a security currency or other asset in markets in which there are differences in price. In aiming to profit from the price difference, the arbitrageur helps to eliminate it.

Articles of Association. A set of international regulations for running a company or a concern. According to the Indian Companies Act, the articles of association must be registered when the company is formed.

Articulated Accounts. Refers to the accounts in which the profit and loss account (income statement) and the balance sheet form part of the same Double Entry system, so that the residual balance on the former matches the changes in owner's equity in the latter.

A Shares. A term often used for non-voting Ordinary Shares.

Assets. Refers to the property of a business; they may be classified as:

(a) Current Assets, consisting of cash, stock and book debts;

(b) Fixed Assets, consisting of buildings, plant and machinery;

(c) Intangible Assets, being the value of goodwill or patents.

Assets/Employee Ratio. Refers to a ratio which is used as an indication of the capital intensity of a company; the ratio has been found to be useful for comparing the capital of companies within an industry group.

Asset Stripping. The term used for identifying and selling off the easily separable assets of a company that has been the object of a successful Takeover Bid.

Asset Valuation. Attaching prices to Assets and more especially to Non-Monetary Assets.

Assurance. Payment of a premium at regular intervals so that at a particular time a fixed amount may become due for repayment to the person concerned. For e.g. life assurance, endowment assurance.

At a Discount. At a price which is lower than par value, or lower than normal, because of special circumstances.

At Par. The nominal value of a share. When a share is issued at par it is available for purchase at the value mentioned on the share, for e.g. Rs. 10/- share may be issued and may be available for purchase at Rs. 10/-. But the market value of the share may be either higher or lower.

At a Premium. At a price which is higher than par value, or higher than normal, because of special circumstances.

Attachment. Prevention of disposal of specific goods or money by a debtor through an order of the court, so that the money or property may be available in future for the settlement of the debts.

Attributes Sampling. In an audit or quality control context, sampling which is based on the qualitative rather than the monetary characteristics of sampling units.

Attrition. In labour economics it refers to the wastage of a labour force that occurs naturally because of voluntary quits, retirements, discharges for cause, and deaths.

Auction. Offer of goods for sale in public. Generally the goods are to be sold on the spot to the highest bidder.

Audit. In general, this term refers to the mechanism within the process of Accountability whereby the performance of those in control of the resources of an organization is checked or monitored by or on behalf of interested parties.

Audit By Rotation. Refers to a process of systematically auditing aspects of a company's financial or general performance on a cyclical basis. The period between audits is termed as an audit cycle.

Audit Evidence. Information which is obtained by an auditor in arriving at the conclusions on which he bases his opinion on financial statements.

Auditing Standards. Refers to the standards designed to give credibility to the independence, objectivity and technical skill of auditors.

Audit Opinion. Refers to the opinion which is expressed by an auditor upon financial statements.

Audit Programme. A description of the work to be done in an audit, serving both as a planning document and as a control on procedures carried out.

Audit Report. A report made by an auditor upon financial statements.

Audit Sample. Refers to a check of part only of the accounting records under the secruting of an auditor.

Audit Trial. Refers to the impact of a transaction through all the relevant stages of an accounting system.

Autarky. A policy of self-sufficiency, whereby a country attempts to be as independent as possible of imports from other countries.

Authorised Capital. The amount of capital mentioned in the memorandum of association of a company. The company cannot issue shares for more than the authorised capital, unless certain formalities are fulfilled.

Authorized minimum Share Capital. The minimum share capital permitted for a public company.

Authorized Share Capital. The maximum amount of Share Capital which a Company Limited by Shares has authority to issue.

Automated Policy. Refers to a reliance on fixed rates of change in money and tax rates, rather than frequent discretionary changes in monetary or fiscal policy to influence the level of economic activity.

Automatic Saving. If a person's net income has been too large to spend, the unspent income is known as automatic saving.

Automatic Stabilizers. Those elements of the economic system, both private and public, which tend to correct recessionary or inflationary tendencies.

Automation. A term applied to any machine process that is automatically controlled, and also to the use of computers which carry out intricate calculations in a very short time. One example of automation is a continuous electronically controlled production line which links together a number of machines, each performing a single operation automatically.

Autonomous Expenditures. Refer to expenditures exogenous to a madel which are used to forecast Gross National Product.

Autonomous Investment. Investment which is not influenced by such economic factors as the rate of interest, the rate of growth of sales, or the rate of return on investment.

Autonomous Spending. Refers to the spending that has been found to be independent of the level of income and interest rates.

Average Collection Period. Refers to the speed at which a company collects its debts. It can be calculated as average.

$$\frac{\text{debtors} \times 365 \text{ days}}{\text{credit sales}}$$

Average Cost (average total unit cost). The total costs divided by the number of units produced at the point under consideration.

Average Cost Pricing. A pricing rule according to which firms add a mark-up onto average variable costs (AVC) so as to cover its average total costs. Hence price (P) may be put as follows:

$$P = AVC + GPM = AC$$

where GPM denotes the gross profit margin make-up and is comprised of an overhead element and a fixed net profit margin thought 'normal' or 'fair' for industry.

Average Due Date. Refers to the date on which a single amount can be paid in lieu of several payments on different dates.

Average Fixed Cost. The total of those costs of a business that do not vary with the amount of business done, divided by the number of units produced at the point under consideration.

Average Propensity to Consume. The proportion of income, Y that is spent on consumption, C. The average propensity to consume = C/Y. It may be stated as a propensity to consume out of either national income or disposable income.

Average Propensity to Save. The proportion of income, Y that is saved, S. The average propensity to save = S/Y. It may be stated as a propensity to save out of either national income or disposable income.

Average Rate of Tax. Refers to the amount which is paid in tax as a percentage of income received during a given period.

Average Revenue (per unit). The total revenue from the sale of a given quantity of the same good divided by the number of units sold. Thus average revenue per unit is equal to price per unit.

As total revenue will consist of price x quantity (P.X.) then we have

$$AR = \frac{A.X}{X} = P$$

Average Revenue Product. Refers to the average physical product of an input (factor of production) multiplied by the average revenue.

Average Variable Cost. The total of those costs of a business that vary with the amount of business done, divided by the number of units produced at the point under consideration.

Average Rate of Tax (also known as effective rate of tax). Usually taken to mean total income tax payments as a proportion of income. The definition of income normally means the gross income, i.e. before allowances.

Avoidable Costs. Costs that may be saved by not adopting a given alternative.

B

Back Duty. Refers to the tax payable on income undisclosed at the time earned.

Backed Note. A receiving note which is endorsed by a shipbroker and authorizing the master of a ship to take on board water-borne goods. It is evidence that freight has been or will be paid.

Back Freight. Freight which is payable when delivery is not taken within a reasonable time at the port of discharge and the master, who has implied power to do so, deals with the goods at the owner's expense, probably by transferring them to another port.

Back-Haul Rates. The cheap rates normally given for cargoes on ships, which would be returning in ballast to pick up a new cargo. The overhead costs are assigned mainly to the outward journey and the backhaul rate can be kept cheaper because only direct costs must be met and any return in excess of these is clear profit.

Backlog Depreciation. Refers to the under-provision that arises when the amount of accumulated depreciation recorded for a fixed tangible asset has been inadequate to cover the cost of its replacement.

Back-to-back. A reference to offsetting loans, generally made in one currency in one country against a loan in another currency in another country; it is involving two parties, matching assets and liabilities in opposite directions.

Bad. Means a commodity or product which produces disutility for its consumer.

Bad Debt. An amount owing which is not expected to be received and is therefore written off either to a bad debts account or to a previously established provision for bad (or doubtful) debts.

Bailment. Possession of goods belonging to another. It may voluntary as in the case of borrowing or involuntary as in the case of some article found in one's premises accidentally.

Balance. The term used for the difference between two sides of an Account. It is entered on the lesser side to make both sides equal and then brought down to the opposite side.

Balanced Budget. A budget is said to be a balanced budget when current income exactly equals current expenditure.

Balanced-budget Multiplier. Refers to the ratio of the change in real income to the change in government expenditure if government expenditure and tax revenues get changed by equal amounts.

Balanced Growth. In growth theory it refers to a dynamic condition of an economy where all real variables have been growing at the same constant proportional rate (which have been zero or negative).

Balance of Indebtedness. The balance of indebtedness of a country is a statement of the total claims of its residents on foreign countries and the total claims of residents of toreign countries on its residents. While the balance of payments covers a period of time, the balance of indebtedness relates to a given point in time.

Balance of Payments. Refers to the relation between the payments of all kinds made from one country to the rest of the world and its receipts from all other countries.

Balance of Trade. Refers to the relationship between the values of a country's imports and its exports, i.e. the 'visible' balance.

Balance Sheet. A statement of accounts, generally prepared at the end of financial year. The statement shows the assets and liabilities of a concern separately.

Balance Sheet Formats. Methods of presenting the items in a Balance Sheet.

Balance Sheet Identity. Synonym for Accounting Identity.

Balance Sheet Total. In general, the total of the two halves of a Balance Sheet, however drawn up.

Balancing Item. An item which gets entered in the balance of payments accounts to make the account balance.

Bancor. The name assigned by Keynes to an international currency which he proposed has to be created by an international bank, used for setting international debts and which would constitute part of international liquidity.

Bank. Refers to a financial intermediary which accepts funds, principally as deposits repayable on demand or at short notice, and which it to make advances by overdrafts and loans, and by discounting bills, and to hold other, mainly financial assets like marketable securities.

Bank Advance. A loan given by a bank against security. The interest rate is fixed according to the agreement between the parties.

Bank Bill. A bill which has been accepted by an accepting house, a clearing bank, or one of banks on behalf of a customer for whom an acceptance credit has been opened.

Bank Cheque. A cheque in which no sum of money is written. The holder is expected to fill in the amount himself.

Bank Confirmation. Refers to a request by an auditor to a bank to confirm details of an audit client's bank accounts, assets of the client held by the bank, and other financial information.

Bank Credit. Refers to the lending by the banking system, by whatever means: bank advances, discounting bills or purchasing securities.

Bank Deposits. The funds deposited in bank accounts. In reality they have been simply records of indebtedness on a bank to the depositor, and they arise from the character of banks as financial intermediaries.

Bankers Cheque. A Cheque drawn by one bank on another, either for clearing purposes or for transferring customer's money.

Banking Panic. The terms used for an episode in which a failure of confidence in one or more banks produced a sudden and wide-spread 'run' by the public on banks in general, to with-draw deposits, or in times when private banknote issues had been common to demand payment of such notes in another medium.

Banking System. Refers to a network of commercial banks co-ordinated, influenced and controlled by statutory regulation and a central bank.

Bank Loan. Any advance by a bank, but there is a distinction in bank lending between overdraft terms and loan term. A bank advance specifically in the form of a loan gets credited in full to the borrower's account at the outset and the interest liability might be a fixed sum calculated on the initial loan 'and its duration. In some cases, e.g. personal and term loans, there occurs provision for repayment by regular instalments.

Bank Notes. The currency notes which are in circulation. Orignally these notes are considered as pieces of paper on which the Central Bank of the country stated that it owed the holder a particular sum of money.

Bank of Issue. A bank, authorised to issue bank notes.

Bank Overdraft. Refers to an overdrawn balance on cash at bank account (a credit balance in the books of an enterprise, a debit balance in the books of a bank and the statement it issues).

Bank Rate. The official rate of interest charged by the Reserve Bank of India as the lender of the last result. It is a rate at which the Reserve Bank of India discounts bills of exchange.

Bank Reconciliation Statement. Refers to a statement reconciling as at a particular date the balance of cash at bank as shown in an enterprise's own records and that indicated on the Bank Statement. In principle the two balances should be equal and opposite.

Bankruptcy. The situation in which a person (individual or concern) is unable to discharge his debt obligations. A court has to declare the person bankrupt according to the law. In the case of bankruptcy the creditors get only proportionate repayment of the debts due to them.

Bank Statement. It is an extract of the customer's account from the point of view of the bank and in principle should disclose a balance equal and opposite to that shown in the customer's cash at bank account in his own ledger.

Bargaining Tariff. The term used for the tariff imposed by a country to strengthen its position in trade negotiations with other countries, when it may be using the promise of reductions in the tariff to obtain trade concessions.

Bargaining Theory of Wages. Wages have been commonly fixed in a collective bargaining process; an arrangement that differs mechanically from the orthodox demand-supply adjustment process. The bargaining theory of wages is referred to model building exercises of the bargaining process applicable to union management relations that seek to proceed beyond the bilateral monopoly model in which the final outcome of bargaining has been indeterminate.

Barter. Refers to a method of exchanging goods and services directly for other goods and services without employing a separate unit of account or medium of exchange.

Barter Agreements. Agreements between countries, usually with balance of payments troubles, for the direct exchange of agreed quantities of goods without the mediation of international finance.

Barter Economy. Refers to an economy where the exchange of goods and services is realised by the method of bartar, which would give rise to very little specialization or division of labour due to the requirement of double-concidence of wants.

Base Drift. The term used for a problem when the money supply of a country grows beyond its nominated ceiling.

Base Rate. Usually, the basic rate for lending by a bank.

Base Stock. In the context of Inventory Valuation, this term refers to the calculation of the cost of inventories (stocks and work in progress) on the basis that a fixed unit value is ascribed to a predetermined number of units of stock, any excess over this number being valued by some other method.

'Basic' Balance of Payments. Refers to that part of a nation's balance of payments which covers the balance on current account and long-term capital flows.

Basic Industries. Iron and steel, fertilizer, machine tools, boilers, etc.

Critical Industries: Coal, power, petroleum, paper, cement, drugs and pharmaceuticals, etc.

Strategic Industries: Arms and ammunition, tomic energy, telephone etc.

Core Industries: Include basic, critical and strategic industries and are under state ownership or control.

Basing-point System. Refers to a type of pricing in which the various sellers in a market agree that the price to be charged for a good has to be calculated by the sum of a fixed price, and an agreed transport change which gets related to the distance between the consumer and the nearest of a number of agreed locations known as 'basing points'.

'Basket of Currency' System of Exchange Value. In this system, the exchange value of the country's currency is fixed taking into account the then prevailing parity values of some major international units of currency. This system is applied to the Indian rupee since 1975.

Bayesian Techniques. The term used for the methods of statistical analysis (including estimation and statistical inference) in which prior information has been formally combined with sample data to produce estimates, or test hypotheses.

Bear. Refers to an investor who sells a stock, bond, currency or commodity in the expectation of a decline in its price and the hope of buying it back at a lower price.

Bear and Bull. Terms used in the stock exchange to refer to individuals or conditions. An individual who sells shares in the belief that prices will fall later is called a bear. The very act of selling shares induces the public to believe that the prices are to crash and thereby causes a fall in the prices of shares. An individual who buys shares in the hope that the shares will appreciate quickly is called a Bull. When the buying spree goes on, the public feel that the prices are likely to rise further. Thus artificial demand is created leading to appreciation in the prices of shares. The condition of a stock exchange is described either as Bearish or as Bullish depending on the situation described above.

Beggar-my-neighbour Policies. The economic measures which are taken by one country to improve its domestic economic conditions, normally to reduce unemployment, and which have adverse effects on other economies.

Below the Line. Refers to that part of the profit and loss account (income statement) below the measure of earnings on which Earnings Per Share (EPS) is based.

Beneficiary. Refers to a person who benefits under a will or a trust.

Benefit Principle. A traditional theory of taxation which may be stated as that tax burdens should be allocated among tax payers in accordance with the benefits they receive from the provision of public goods.

Bertrand's Duopoly Model. Refers to a model of a two firm market developed by J. Bertrand in 1883. The model is different from the Cournot Duopoly model in that each firm has been assumed to maximize profits on the presumption that the other firm will not change its price. Bertrand's model results in a stable equilibrium for the two firms.

Beta. A measure of the Systematic Risk of a company's shares, i.e. the sensitivity of the share price to movements in the market. A share having a beta of 1.0 (a 'neutral' share) will on average move in line with the market. A share with a beta greater than 1.0 (an 'aggressive' share) will on average go up faster in a Bull market and down faster in Bear market. A share having a beta of less than 1.0 (a 'defensive' share) will on average fluctuate less than the market as a whole. Betas change over time but most are reasonably stationary.

Bid. The term used for an offer of payment which an individual or organization makes for possession or control of assets, input, goods or services.

Bilateral Exchange Rate. The term used for a conventional concept of a currency exchange rate, such as the dollar price of sterling yen, or Deutsche marks.

Bilateral Monopoly. Refers to a market structure in which single seller faces a single buyer.

Bilateral Oligopoly. Refers to a market situation in which a few sellers confront a few buyers.

Bilateral Trade. Trade between two countries, strictly interpreted the value of the goods and services exported by country A to country B must be exactly matched by the value of the exports from country B to country A.

Bill. A short-term debt instrument which is in the form of a document ordering the drawee (i.e. the debtor) to pay the drawer (the creditor) a stated sum at a specified date, or 'at sight' which means on demand.

Bill Broker. The term used for person who specializes in bringing together, for a commission, buyers and sellers of bills.

Bilan Social. Literally, a social balance sheet.

Bill of Exchange. Refers to an unconditional order in writing addressed by one person to another, signed by the person giving it, requiring the person to whom it gets addressed to pay on demand, or at a fixed or determinable future time, a certain sum in money to, or to the order of, a specified person or to the bearer.

Bill of Lading. Refers to a document which is signed by the master of a ship on behalf of the owners, acknowledging the receipt of goods put on board and setting out the terms and conditions under which the goods will be carried.

B.I.S. The Bank for International Settlements.

Black Market. Any illegal market which has been established in a context where prices have been fixed at minimum or maximum levels, usually by government.

Black-Scholes Option Model. A model which was developed by F. Black and M. Scholes for determining the equilibrium value of an Option given certain assumptions. According to the model the value of an option is a function of the short-term interest rate, of the time to expiration, and of the variance of the rate of return on the shares, but is not a function of the expected return on the shares.

Blue Chip Rate. Refers to the lowest interest rate payable by borrowers having the highest credit rating.

Blue-sky Laws. In the USA, state laws which are governing transactions in securities.

Bond. In general, a fixed interest security, which is issued by a central or local government authority or by a company.

Bond Duration. Refers to the weighted average period of time which get elapsed before the cash flows from a bond are received, the weights used being the present values of the individual cash flows expressed as a fraction of the total present value of the bond.

Bonded Warehouse. Warehouse in which dutiable articles are stored without previously paying duty.

Bond Immunization. Refers to the heding in such a way that the mean duration of bond investments has been set equal to the mean term of the liabilities which the investments are required to satisfy.

Bond Table. Refers to a table in which are set out the yields to maturity of bonds for which is known the coupon rate, the present market price and the value at maturity.

Bonus Issue. An issue of shares to existing share holders in a company made possible by the capitalisation of reveres. No payment is necessary in this case.

Bonus Shares. Shares that result from a Bonus Issue.

Book-keeping. Refers to the systematic recording of financial and economic Transactions and other Events.

Book-Keeping Barter. The term used for a system of Barter in which money is used as a Unit of Account but not, or only infrequently, as a means of payment.

Books of Account. A general term which is used for Ledgers, Journals and other accounting records.

Book Value. The term used for the monetary amount of an asset or a liability as stated in the balance sheet and books of account.

Book Yield. Synonym for Accounting Rate of Return.

Bottom Line. Refers to the line that separates Above the Line from Below the Line and constitutes the measure of earnings on which Earnings Per Share (EPS) is based.

Bought Ledger. Synonym for Creditors Ledger.

Boom. According to the theory of trade cycle the highest point beyond which upward movement is not possible. At this condition prices and employment are at the maximum.

Boulwarism. The process of collective bargaining over terms and conditions of employment has been normally one of compromise and concession; the two parties bargain and approach one another untill a point somewhere between their original or opening positions is realised that is mutually satisfactory to them.

Bourgeois Accounting. Soviet name for accounting as practised in capitalist countries.

Bourgeoisie. Refers to that section of industrial society which came into prominence in the course of the industrial revolution as entrepreneurs and professional persons.

Bourse. French name for a stock exchange of a commodity exchange.

Brain Drain. Means the migration of educated and skilled labour from poorer to richer countries.

Branch Accounting. Accounting for geographically separated sections of enterprises. The accounting system adopted depends upon the degree to which the branch is controlled from its head office.

Branch Banking. Refers to the provisions of banking services through a network of branch offices which are owned by a single banking company.

Break-even Analysis. The costs of producing a good have been splitted into two main parts. Fixed costs have been those that remain the same for the firm however many goods are produced, i.e. rates, rent, etc. Variable costs vary with the number of items produced, i.e. raw materials for the goods labour to produce them, etc. From the cost accountant's point of view, the break-even sales volume may be defined as that which ensures that all fixed and variable costs are covered, given a particular selling price

$$= \frac{\text{Break-even volume Fixed costs}}{\text{Selling price minus variable cost per unit}}$$

'Break-even' Level of Income. The point at which consumption expenditures have been just equal to income. Below this point consumption has been greater than income, that is dis-saving occurs, above this point consumption has been less than income that is saving occurs.

Break-even Chart. Refers to a chart on which are plotted total revenue and total cost (divided into fixed and variable) at various levels of activity. Total revenue and total cost have been assumed to be linear over the Relevant Range of production.

Break-even Point. Refers to the point at which total revenue equals total cost. It can be expressed either in monetary units or in units of products sold.

Broker. One who buys and sells bonds and other financial assets.

Brokerage. A fixed cost which is charged by the broker for each act of investment or encashment of bonds and other financial assets.

Bubble Company. A company that as never done any real business or honest trade. A company formed with an intention of defrauding the public.

Budget. In India Government presents a major budget every year. Traditionally the Budget was the occasion when the Government made changes to the level and structure of taxation.

Budgetary Control. Refers to a system whereby checks have been made on expenditure and revenue flow against targets which have been set out in a budget.

Budget Deficit. An excess of government expenditures; over revenues a negative budget surplus.

Budgeted Cost. A cost which is included in a Budget. It may also be a Standard Cost.

Budget Line. Refers to a line in commodity space which indicates what combinations of goods the consumer is able to buy with a given income. The slope and location of the line have been determined by the prices of the goods in question.

Budget Manual. Refers to a written set of instructions which is serving as rule book and a reference book for a budget programme.

Budget Period. Refers to the period for which a budget is drawn up: typically a year, but longer periods are used for Long Range Planning. An annual budget may be broken down into shorter periods.

Budget Surplus. Current income in excess of current expenditures.

Bufferstock Facility. Refers to a facility extended by the International Monetary Fund for the purposes of providing loans for countries wanting to finance commodity stocks.

Built-in Flexibility. Refers to a feature of tax a system resulting in a rise or fall in tax revenue as national income rises or falls. The most important example has been a progressive income tax which will cause tax revenue to change more than proportionately with changes in national income. Built-in flexibility is reduced by Indexation.

Bull. Refers to an investor who buys a stock, bond, currency or commodity in the expectation of a rise in its price.

Bullet Loan. A single-repayment loan having no amortisation; that is, a loan which has not been paid off in instalments.

Bullion. Precious metals like gold or silver which have been held in bulk in the form of ingots or bars. Gold bullion has been used for international monetary transactions between banks and governments.

Bullion Market. A market in which gold bullion has been bought and sold.

Burden. A synonym for Overhead.

Bureaucracy, Economic Theory of. The model assumes that state agencies will behave as budget maximizers. Large budgets make bureaucrafts to satisfy their preference for salaries, promotion, job security and such non-pecuniary advantages as power, prestige and opportunities to allocate contracts.

Business Behaviour. Refers to those actions or policy strategies pursued by firms with the aim of favourably changing the business conditions they face.

Business Combination. Refers to a general term for the bringing together by acquisition (purchase) or merger (polling or interests) of two or more companies.

Business Finance. Refers to the provision of funds at the time they are needed to assist a business during an adverse period of identity between payment and receipts.

Business Performance. Refers to extent to which an industry achieves the goals or objectives its member firms pursue.

Business Profit. Refers to the sun of Current Cost Operating Profit and realizable Holding Gains

Business Risk. Refers to the Risk which is related to the industry to which an enterprise belongs and to general economic conditions rather than to Gearing (Leverage).

Buy Back. An offsetting purchase to cover or liquidate a short sale.

Buyer Concentration. The extent to which total transactions within a market get dominated by the largest few buyers.

Buyers Market. A market characterized by excess supply in which sellers consequently experience difficulty at selling all their output at anticipated prices.

Buy in. To cover, offset, or close out a short position.

Buying-in. In respect of currency, the buying by a government of its own currency in order to maintain its international value.

Byproduct. A product with relatively insignificant sales value compared with the major product.

C

Call. An amount which is payable on a share subsequent to application and Allotment.

Called-up Share Capital. Refers to the amount of the Issued Share Capital which has been called up, i.e., the amounts the shareholders have been asked to pay to date.

Call Loan. A loan which may be terminated or called at any time by the lender or borrower.

Call Money. Also known as 'money at call and at short notice'. In the balance sheet of a bank, money at call is the money that must be repaid on demand. Money at short notice is the money borrowed for a short duration, generally 24 hours at a low rate of interest. When the money at short notice is available in plenty, it is described as easy money. When it is not so available it is called tight money.

Call-option. Refers to a contract giving the option for buying shares at a future date within a prearranged time limit.

Call to. To buy.

Callable. Refers to a bond issue, all or part of which may be redeemed by the issuing corporation under specified conditions before maturity.

Cambridge School. A view of economics, which has derived from two main intellectual influences.

1. J.M. Keynes who has been regarded as the originator of the Cambridge School.

2. Ricardo and Marx of the classical tradition.

It has been particularly critical of neoclassical economics and of the work of P. Samuelson and R. Solow of the Massachusetts

Institute of Technology (MIT) of Cambridge, USA, who have been seen as its main representatives. This antagonism results in a debate between the two Cambridges that has been continuing from the 1930s to the present with the participants scarcely agreeing on the importance of topics considered or on the techniques of the discussion.

The Cambridge School (England) considers an economic model as encompassing, historical, sociological and psychological notions and facts as well as the purely economic. In its attack on neoclassical economics, a principal target involves the use of the aggregate production function, especially in growth theory. Some of the more noteworthy members of the school have been Mrs. J. Robinson. N. Kaldor, Lord Khan, L. Pasinetti and P. Sraffa. The influence is also to Italy where P. Gareguani, D.M. Nuti and L. Spavanta have been associated with the work of the school.

Cambridge Theory of Money. It is a 'cash balance' form of the quantity theory of money. It has been developed by Cambridge economists like Marshall. Pigou and Robertson (the early Cambridge School) and contained in the equation:

$$M = kPT$$

where M represents the amount of money (bank deposits); k represents the reciprocal of the velocity of circulation; P represents the general price level; and T represents the value of output. If the velocity of circulation of money becomes four times in a given period, then k will be one-quarter of expenditure; k is the proportion of the community's expenditure on goods and services which on average is held as cash during the period.

Capacity Utilization. Refers to the ratio of actual to potential output. It refers to firms, industries or whole economies and gives a measure of the amount of the total capacity that is being used.

Capital. It may be defined as 'wealth which is used for the production of further wealth; or simply a commodity which is used in the production or other goods and services, e.g. such as plant or equipment. It represents current consumption forgone in order to obtain future production and future consumption; it enhances the productivity of labour and land.

Issued Capital. The amount of capital actually issued by the company. The capital is normally issued by a company in the form of shares.

Share Capital. The total of shares issued are authorised to be issued by a company. The shares may be ordinary shares or preference shares.

Paid-up Capital. That part of the capital of a company, which is called up and paid-up.

Capital Accumulation. Means an increase in manmade equipment like machinery, tools, buildings and other structures, and stocks of goods, used, for or capable of being used for the production of goods and services.

Capital Allowances. Refer to the deductions from gross business profits for the purpose of covering the depreciation of assest which are allowed by the tax authorities when calculating taxable income.

Capital Asset. The term used for an asset, which is not bought or sold as part of the everyday running of a business. Examples include property, land, or shares in another company.

Capital Asset Pricing Model (CAPM). Refers to a model of the securities market which is based on Portfolio analysis. According to the CAPM the expected return in equilibrium on any risky asset in a perfect capital market is given by:

$$\bar{R}_j = i + (\bar{R}_m - i)\,\beta_i$$

where $\bar{R}_j$ refers to the expected rate of return for security *j*. $\bar{R}_m$ is the expected rate of return for the Market Portfolio, *i* refers to the risk-free rate of return and β_i(Beta) is a measure of the Systematic Risk of security *j*.

Capital-authorised, Nominal or Registered. Synonymous terms for capital fixed by the Memorandum of Association of a company.

Capital Budgeting. The process of allocating investible funds to capital projects. Many techniques are used for this purpose. There are traditional accountants' methods like payback period and rate of return on capital employed.

Capital Charges. The charges which companies and individuals are making in their accounts for interest payments on capital borrowed, depreciation of assets and loan repayments.

Capital Coefficients. It is another name for the capital-output ratio.

Capital Consumption. Refers to a measure of depreciation which is used in National Income And Expenditure Accounts and based on current replacement costs.

Capital Controversy. The term used for a debate between the Cambridge School (centred in Cambridge University, England) and the Neoclassical School, of the Massachusetts Institute of Technology, Cambridge, Massachusetts; about the validity or otherwise of the neoclassical approach to economics. Debate has centred mainly on the correct concept of capital to use and its place, if any, in an aggregate production function. The possibility of a reswitching of techniques argued forcefully by the Cambridge School has been sufficient to render invalid many of the assumptions of neoclassical economic theory (especially neoclassical growth theory). The debates some what ceased because the Cambridge School (England) consider their view as proved.

The neoclassical school while accepting that reswitching weakens economic theories derived from assumptions which are unsustainable, do not accept that neoclassical theory should be abandoned in totality.

Capital Cost Component. In relation to the total production cost of each unit of output, the capital cost component is given by:

$$\frac{\text{Capital Charges}}{\text{Units of Output}}$$

where the capital charges have been the sum of the annual interest charges on capital employed and the annual depreciation charges, and the units of output relate to the year under consideration.

Capital Cost of. The cost of obtaining the total capital employed by a business, expressed as a rate of interest.

Capital Employed. The term used for the capital in use in a business it consists of the total assets minus the current liabilities.

Capital Employed, Return on. The relating of profit to the estimate of average capital employed to yield a ratio, commonly called the primary ratio, as follows:

$$\frac{\text{Profit}}{\text{Capital}}$$

Capital Expenditure. Expenditure of a non-recurrent nature resulting in the acquisition of assets.

Capital Gain. Refers to the difference between the purchase price of an asset and its resale price at some later date, where that difference has been positive.

Capital Gains Tax. A tax which is levied on the capital appreciation of property. In most countries capital gains are not classed as income but they confer purchasing power and so have been fit subject of taxation.

Capital Goods. Goods which are made for the purpose of producing consumer goods and other capital goods, e.g., machinery of all kinds. This term is synonymous with 'producer goods'.

Capital Intensity. The ratio of capital to labour employed in production.

Capital-intensive Economy. Refers to an economy in which the majority of production techniques have been capital-intensive. Most advanced countries have this property.

Capital-intensive Industry. Refers to industry in which the ratio of capital input to labour input has been higher than the average ratio for industry as a whole. The capital input could be found out by the depreciation costs of plant and equipment.

Capital-intensive Sector. Refers to a sector in an economy where the majority of production techniques have been capital-intensive in nature. The industrial sectors in less developed countries have been usually capital-intensive.

Capital-intensive Techniques. The term used for a production technique which is having a higher proportion of capital than any other factor of production.

Capital Investment. Refers to an investment in Fixed Assets.

Capital Investment Appraisal. Refers to the appraisal of capital investment projects to determine which should be selected. A capital project can be regarded as a set of expected incremental cash flows.

Capitalisation. It can refer to the composition of a company's long term sources of funds, i.e., its Capital Structure, or to the total market value of its issued shares (Market Capitalization). The term can refer to the process of obtaining a Net Present Value by applying on annuity or perpetuity formula to future earnings or cash flows.

Capital Lease. US term for Finance Lease.

Capitalised Value. The value which would be place on an asset if it were to produce its existing earnings as current market rates of interest.

Capitalism. Refers to a political, social and economic system in which property including capital assets have been owned controlled to a large extent by private persons.

Capital Issue. The issue of shares in a company by issuing the prospectus. It may also be done by means of introduction, offer for sale or tender.

Capitalist Development, Schumpeter's Theory of. A theory developed by Professor J.A. Schumpeter (1883-1950). This theory starts from the circular flow of economic life where producers and consumers all function in a state of equilibrium, all adjustments and adaptations having been made, into this circular flow Schumpeter introduces a shift in the production function which generates a sequence of alterations in the behaviour of economic actors—bank credit expands and eventually a secondary wave of investment activity gets imposed on top of the primary wave as the expectations of the enlarged business community have been influenced by the evidence and by the consequences of business expansion.

Capital Labour Ratio. Refers to the ratio at which labour and capital have been combined within the production process. Generally labour and capital have been measured as flows per unit of time.

Capital Labour Substitution. The term used for the process of changing the factor proportions of capital and labour in a production technique, if one factor costs less than the other, there will exist a tendency for the expensive factor to get substituted by the cheaper one in a free market situation.

Capital Levies. Once-for-all capital taxes. Death duties are a form of capital levy.

Capital Maintenance Concept. Refers to a concept in which income results only after capital has been maintained.

Capital Market. A market comprising institutions which are involved in the purchase and sale of securities, e.g., the new issue market and the stock exchange.

Capital Market Instruments. Financial instruments like company shares and bonds, long-term government bonds, and local government bonds.

Capital Market Line. Refers to a line which expresses graphically all the available combinations of the Market Portfolio with riskless borrowing and lending.

Capital Movements. Refer to international flows of funds which may be undertaken by either private individuals or governments. An important element in the Balance of Payments.

Capital Output Ratio. Means the ratio of the amount of capital to the amount of output produced by that capital. A constant capital output ratio is forming the basis of the accelerator principle.

Capital Rationing. A situation where there has been a budgetary constraint on the amount of funds available for investment in projects over and above the normal market constrain determined by the relationship between cost of capital and expected returns.

Capital Recovery. Refers to the process by which the original investment in a physical asset has been recovered over its economic life. In the absence of inflation, capital recovery has been achieved through depreciation allowances.

Capital Redemption Reserve. The term used for an undistributable reserve arising from the redemption of shares or the purchase by a company of its own shares.

Capital Reserve. The company accounting, a Reserve that is not distributable as a matter of law, prudence, or business policy.

Capital Stock. The aggregate or sum of capital goods in an economy. This implies that the stock of capital can be measured by a single number, and needs the heroic assumption that the diverse constituents of this stock (factories, roads, tools, etc.) can be reduced to a common unit and summed to get on unambiguous measure of society's physical stock of capital.

Capital Structure. Refers to the composition of an enterprise's sources of funds, especially long term.

In practice capital structure is influenced by such factors as the relative costs of the various sources of capital the amount and stability of earnings, the risk of insolvency, dividend policy and a desire to retain control.

Capital, Theory of. An area of economic theory concerned with the analysis of the formation of capital, the role of inputs, the role of time and intertemporal planning, and the mechanism of resource allocation between consumption and investment.

Capital Transactions. The leading or borrowing of sums of money, or the transfer of assets accumulated in the past.

Capital Transfer Tax. Refers to a tax on transfers of wealth, whether or not occurring at the date of death.

Capital Widening. Refers to the process of accumulating capital at the same rate as the growth of the labour force so that the capital—labour ratio remains constant.

Capitation Tax. Also known as a poll tax. It is a tax which is levied on each member of the community equally irrespective of wealth or income.

Captive Market. The term used for a market in which the supplier of a good or service has been in a monopolistic position, the consumer being unable to get suitable substitutes or to do without. For many years, the gas industry, using no other raw material save coal, was a captive market.

Capture Theory. A theory of regulation which was developed by George Stigler. Basically, an industry that is regulated can benefit from its regulation by 'capturing' the regulatory agency involved. This can take place because of political influence superior technical knowledge that forces the regulatory agency to depend on the industry; appointees being selected from the regulated industry or the possibility of future positions in the industry and the agency's need for recognition and informal co-operation from the industry.

Carat. This unit used for measuring the refinement of gold. Pure gold is assigned 24 carat. 18 carat gold will have 18 parts gold and 6 parts alloy.

Cardinalism. Refers to the doctrine that utility has been measurable in cardinal units.

Cardinal Utility 1. The utility attached to a bundle of goods is capable of absolute measurement in terms of some units like 'utils' (a term used for example by Jevons in his Theory of Political Economy in 1871) which would be comparable to the units used for height, weight, and distance.

2. It relates only to the intervals between utility levels. Thus, faced with four situations 1, 2, 3 and 4, if a consumer can sav that

the difference between the utility levels of 1 and 2 is some multiple or fraction of the difference between the utility levels of 3 and 4, he can be said to have scaled his utility levels in cardinal terms.

Carrying. A general term which is used for both borrowing and lending which is on commodity futures markets.

Carrying Charge. Charges which are associated with the storage of a commodity, e.g., warehouse charges insurance and other incidentals often including an interest charge and estimated values in respect of the loss or gain in weight.

Cartel. Means the formal agreement between firms in an oligopolistic market to co-operate with regard to agreed procedures on such variables as price and output.

Cartel Sanctions. Refer to the penalties which are imposed by members of a cartel to induce adherence to the joint goals of the group.

Cash Book. Refers to a book of account having a record of cash receipts and cash payments. Receipts and payments not made through a bank are normally made through a separate Petty Cash Book.

Cash Budget. Refers to a plan of future cash receipts and payments based on specified assumptions about such items as sales growth, credit terms, issue of new capital and sales and purchases of fixed assets.

Cash Cow. Refers to a profitable product having a low market growth rate of which a company has a high market share.

Cash Crops. This term is used for crops grown by peasant farmers specifically for sale in the market as opposed to crops directly consumed for subsistence purposes.

Cash Discount. The discount given by creditor on an account paid before the due date. This is done to encourage quick payment.

Cash Economy. Refers to a sector of the economy in which individual tradesmen, trade terms, or small builders, deal directly with customers for cash or cash cheques; customers may include other tradesmen, builders or subcontractors.

Cash Flow. Refers to the sum of retained earnings and depreciation provision made by firms. As such it has been the source of internally generated long term funds available to the company.

Cash Flow Accounting (CFA). Refers to the measuring and recording the financial activities and performance of an enterprise in cash terms.

Cash Flow Forecast. Synonym for Cash Budget.

Cash in Hand System. Refers to a system in which workers have not been paid on, say, an hourly basis for labour only, receiving cash in payment on which income tax has not or will not be paid.

Cashless Society. Refers to a society either so primitive that exchanges through barter alone, or so controlled that goods and services are provided on vouchers only, or sophisticated through the use of credit cards and instant debiting that bank notes and cash become redundant.

Cash Limit System. The system whereby government spending in specified areas gets limited by the amount of cash allocated rather than in real terms.

Cash Management. Refers to the management of the cash balances of an enterprise in such a fashion as to maximize the availability of cash and of investment income on cash not invested in fixed assets or inventories and also so as to avoid the risk of Insolvency.

Cash Market. The term used for a market for the immediate delivery of, and payment for, commodities.

Cash Payments Journal. A Journal which is recording payments of cash out of an enterprise's bank account.

Cash Price. Refers to the price in the market place for a cash commodity (or spot commodity) to get delivered through normal market channels.

Cash Ratio. For a bank, the ratio between cash and deposits.

Cask Receipts Journal. A Journal which is recording receipts of cash into an enterprise's bank account.

Cash Settlement. Refers to a procedure for settlement of contracts by automatic close-out at a cash price which is designated by the clearing house in futures markets which make no provision for delivery, e.g., U.S. dollars.

Casual Employment. Refers to the state of being employed on an ad hoc basis without regular hours or a wage contract.

Caveat Emptor. A Latin legal term meaning 'let the buyer beware'. This maxim expects a buyer to use commonsense in choosing the right type of goods.

Ceiling. Refers to the limit upward growth of output in trade cycle theory. The ceiling will be reached when all factors of production have been utilized at their full capacity output levels.

Central Bank. The institution which is charged primarly with controlling a country's money and banking system, though with other functions depending on the financial structure and environment.

Centralization of Reserves. The name which is given to plants proposing the location of reserves of currency and gold with a central international institution.

Central Limit Theorem. It states that the sum (and mean) of a set of random variables will follow a normal distribution if the sample has been sufficiently large, regardless of the distribution from which the individual variables come.

Certificate of Deposit. A document which is issued by a bank acknowledging a deposit of money with it and constituting a promise to repay that sum, to the bearer, at a specified future date.

Cestui Que Trust. Refers to the person who has the beneficial interest or enjoyment of property, the legal ownership of which is vested in the trustee.

Ceteris Paribus. A Latin expression which means 'other things being equal', Economic analysis, frequently takes place by considering the effect of varying one or a few independent variables while other things remain unchanged. To indicate that this is being done, the term ceteris paribus is used.

Chairman's Statement (review). Refers to a statement which is made by a chairman of a company at its annual general meeting and often included in the Annual Report.

Characteristic Line. Refers to the linear relationship between the return on a security and the return on the Market Portfolio. The slope of the characteristic line would give the Beta of the security.

Characteristics Theory. Generally it is associated with consumer demand theory and the work of K. Lancaster. The basic idea has been that consumers do not demand products but the characteristics of products.

Charge Account. Refers to a credit facility which is extended by retail traders to customers.

Charge and Discharge Account. Refers to an account in which, under properly analysed heads, a person charges himself with certain sums or estate he or she should receive, and in the discharge, credits himself or herself with the sums paid away.

Charity Accounts. The financial statements published by charities.

Chartered Accountant. An Accountancy Bodys.

Charter Party. Refers to a contract to convey goods by sea to a special place for a stated sum.

Chartism. Refers to the use of past patterns of share price movements in an attempt to predict future prices.

Chart of Accounts. Refers to a list of all the account in an enterprise's Ledger or ledgers, constructed in accordance with the scheme of classification adopted by the enterprise.

Cheap Money. Money is said to be cheap when credit is easily available and interest rates are low.

Cheque. A document which is normally supplied in printed form by a bank, ordering the bank to transfer funds from the drawer's current account to a named payee. If the payee signs the reverse side of a cheque it becomes 'negotiable', i.e. he may assign his claim in it to someone else simple by handing it over. A cheque 'crossed' with two lines and bearing the words 'and Co' effectively can be paid only by being credited to a bank account; it should not get paid in cash over a bank's counter.

Cheque Card. Cards which are issued by banks to current account customers, and guarantee the payment of cheques drawn by these customers up to specified limits.

Chernoff Faces. Multidimensional graphics in the form of faces. They are used for displaying relationships between variables such as financial ratios.

Chicago School. Name assigned to a group of economists who, among other things, believe that changes in the money supply have been a major determinant of short-run changes in the level of economic activity, and the most important of the policy instruments available to a federal or national government for affecting short-run changes in economic activity.

C.I.F. Cost, insurance and freight. Term used of goods shipped where the price includes shipping and insurance charges.

Circular Flow of Income. Refers to the flow of payments and receipts between domestic firms and domestic households. Money will pass from households to firms in return for goods and services produced by firms and money passes from firms to households in return for the factor services provided by households.

Circulating Assets. Obsolete term for Current Assets.

Classical Dichotomy. Means the separate and independent determination of relative and absolute prices in classical and neoclassical economics.

Classical Economics. Deals the economic thought of the period from the mid eighteenth to the mid nineteeth century, of which the great bulk emerged from the UK. The major practitioners were Smith, Ricardo, Malthus, Say, Senior and J.S. Mill.

Classical Real Wage Doctrine. Refers to a doctrine which holds that, in the long-run, there exists no trade-off between unemployment and price increases as is implied by the Phillips Curve: it has been taken to indicate that a rising price level will not affect permanently the level of unemployment.

Classical School. See Classical Economics.

Clean Float. Means completely free floating exchange rate with which monetary authorities never interfere.

Clearing House. The place where the different banks in a city or town come together to clear the cheques drawn on various banks and their branches.

Clientele Effect. The term used for the attraction of shareholders to companies which have a Dividend Policy which is suited to their needs.

Closed Economy. A concept which is used mainly in theoretical models to describe an economy having no external trade, which will be completely self-sufficient and insulated from external forces.

Closing Entries. Entries which are made at balance sheet date to close off revenue and expense accounts to the profit and loss account.

Cluster Sampling. In an audit context. Refers to a method of drawing a sample in which the auditor chooses one or more clusters (of, for example, files of invoices or pages of a ledger) at random and then examines all the items within the clusters.

Cobwed Theorem. Refers to the simplest form of a dynamic model in which the supply of a good in year *t* has been a function of the goods price in year *t-1* and where, in any period, price is adjusted so as to clear the market. Such examples may take place in agriculture where the decision to grow a crop or breed, certain animals for food may be based on conditions in previous years. The effect could be 'to generate a process of fluctuating prices, with the fluctuations being 'damped' so as to converge on an equilibrium of prices or 'antidamped' so as to continue fluctuating from one period to the next.'

Codicil. Refers to a supplement to a wall, and forming part of it, generally for the purpose of making some addition or alteration.

Cognitive Complexity. Human Information Processing (HIP).

Coinage. Refers to that part of the hand-to-hand currency that is having metallic coins. Coins have been pieces of metal, normally shaped and stamped which a device which is evidence of their value and of their legal status as money.

Collective Good or Service. A good or service like defence, from which the benefits accrue to all or none.

Collateral Security. Means any security (other than personal security such as a guarantee) taken by a bank when it tends to make an advance to a borrowing customer, and which it is entitled to claim in the event of default.

Comfort Letter. A letter from reporting accountants in which they confirm statements by directors in a prospectus regarding the sufficiency of working capital and other financial matters. A comfort letter is addressed to the issuing house or stockbroker concerned. It is not published in the prospectus.

Coming Out Price. Refers of the price at which new shares are issued.

Command Economy. An economic system which is dominated by central planning, as distinct from a free enterprise economy with a minimum of state interference. Command economy characteristics are not restricted to socialist economies.

Commerce. Also, trade. Buying and selling goods and services, particularly on large scale, between firms communities, states or nations.

The term refers to all those activities which are necessary to transfer commodities and services from the place of their origin to the places of their consumption.

Commercial Banks. A general term denoting those banks, which conduct a general rather than a specialized type of business. They accept deposits on varying terms, but including demand deposits; and their lending to private sector business for non-fixed capital purposes, generally accounts for the grater part of their assets.

Commercial Bill. A bill which is drawn tc finance trade or other commercial or production activities. It has been distinguished from a Treasury Bill or local government bill which have been instruments of public financial operations.

Commercial Paper. A collective term for commercial bills.

Commercial Paper Market. A non-bank short term money market in which corporations lend their surplus cash directly to each other, cutting out intermediate financial institutions.

Commercial Policy. The rules which are adopted by a country for the conduct or regulation of its foreign trade and payments.

Commitments for Capital Expenditure. Amounts to which a company has committed itself in respect of future expenditure on fixed assets.

Committed Costs. Refer to fixed costs that arise from having fixed assets and an organization, e.g., depreciation, rates, long term lease rentals.

Commodities. Objects which are produced because of the process of production, Goods and services.

Commodity Exchange. Refers to a market for the open, competitive, bulk sale and purchase of commodities including financial instruments, for immediate and forward delivery often in the form of a futures contract.

Commodity Futures Contract. Refers to a legally binding commitment to buy or sel! a precisely defined quantity and

quality of a commodity in a given month, the price of which is determined by the participants at the time of transaction.

Commodity Money. Refers to an object used as money which has been also a saleable commodity in its own right: the obvious example has been gold.

Common Costs. Costs of facilities and services which are being shared by a number of departments.

Common External Tariff. A tariff which is applied by members of a customs union, common market or economic commodity at an agreed, similar rate on imports from non-members.

Common law. The law of the land which is crystallised into definite rules from the ancient times. President is the main criterion for common law.

Common Market. In addition to the Common external tariff and the concerted commercial policy of the customs union, a common market is aiming at a unified market area with the free movement of goods, services and factors of production.

Common Pricing. Means the fixing of identical prices for goods by agreement between otherwise competing firms selling through wholesale or retail channels of distribution.

Common Stock. US term for Ordinary Shares.

Communism. In the strict sense it refers to a stage of economic development which is said to take place when all classes in society have been absorbed into the proletariat. In this ideal society the state would have withered away and each person would contribute according to ability and receive according to needs. This utopia envisaged by Marx has been seen to be the stage of economic development which follows on from capitalism and socialism.

Company. A corporate body which is established by individuals under the Indian Companies Act. In the case of an unlimited company, all members are liable for debts. In the case of a limited company, the liability of each member is limited to his share in the company. A private company is one which restricts the right to transfer its shares and as not more than 50 members and cannot invite the public to subscribe for shares. All other companies are public companies. A public company may issue shares and the shareholder has the right to transfer the shares.

Company Limited by Guarantee. A company which is having the liability of its members limited by the memorandum of association to such amount as the members respectively undertake to contribute to the assets of the company in the event of its being wound up.

Company Limited by Share. A company which is having the liability of its members limited by the memorandum of association to the amount, if any, unpaid on the shares respectively held by them.

Company Savings. Refers to that part of firms profits which has been neither paid out in taxes nor distributed to shareholders as dividends.

Company Taxation, The Economist's Canons of. The Economist's criteria for a good company tax have been as follows.

(a) It should be easy and cheap to administer and to comply with;

(b) It should not distort firms' investment and fund raising decisions;

(c) The burden of the tax should be eased according to companies' ability to pay; and

(d) Tax liabilities should be clear-cut.

Comparative Advantage, Theory of. In international trade it refers to a statement that countries tend to specialise in the production of those goods and services which they are able to make or provide most profitably.

Comparative Cost Method. Refers to a method of comparing the profitability of alternative projects. The method takes into consideration the initial cost of alternative projects only it is possible to use this method only where the output and life of each competing scheme is the same.

Comparative Dynamics. The term used for a method employed in dynamic economics with a special feature that the rates of change in the values of the parameters and in the equilibrium values of the variables have been constant.

Compensated Demand Curves. Refer to a demand curve in which the income effect of a price change has been netted out so that, along the demand curve real income has been held constant. The demand curve then exhibits the shape it does because of the substitution effect only.

Competitive Market. Refers to a market in which a very large number of small buyers and sellers trade independently, and as such no one trader is able so significantly influence price.

Complement. Refers to a good which tends to be purchased when another good gets purchased because it 'complements' the first good.

Complete Markets. Refers to a situation in which markets exist for all commodities and claims and hence a market price for any commodity or claim is publicly observable.

Compliance Audit. Refers to an audit whose function has been to test whether statutory obligations (e.g. to present a True and Fair View of or to present fairly a company's financial affairs) have been complied with rather than to test whether a company or other entity is being managed efficiently, effectively and economically.

Compliance Costs. Refers to the costs to the private sector of complying with tax, company and other legislation.

Compliance Tests. Refers to the auditing tests the purposes of which are to obtain evidence that internal control procedures are being applied as presented and thus to indicate the necessary level of Substantive Tests.

Composite Commodity Theorem. This theorem states that if there exists a set of goods whose relative prices (i.e. the price of any on relative to the price of anyother) do not change than those goods can be treated as if they had been one commodity, the so-called composite commodity.

Composite Rate. The rate at which building societies and banks deduct tax from interest paid to depositors.

Compound Discount. Refers to the difference between a future sum (S) and its present value (P), i.e., if S = 1,

$$(1 + i)^n — (1 + i)^n,$$

where i = the compound rate of interest per period and n = the number of periods. The compound rate of discount per period (d) can be calculated as follows:

$$d = \frac{i}{(1 + i)}$$

Compound Interest. The procedure whereby future interest has been paid on past interest earned. Thus if a sum of Rs. 1 is invested at a rate of interest r, its value after one year will be Rs. (1 + r). If the interest gained is now removed, the Rs. 1 will remain and will gather r percent again in the following year. If however the Rs. (1 + r) is left to secure interest, then it will secure interest in the second year of Rs. (1 + r) r, and the original (Rs. (1 + r) will remain. The total investment at the end of the second year will therefore be

$$\text{Rs. } (1 + r) + \text{Rs. } (1 + r)\, r$$

which reduces to

$$\text{Rs. } (1 + r)(1 + r) = \text{Rs. } (1 + r)^2$$

At the end of year t, the investment will have a value of

$$\text{Rs. } (1 + r)^t.$$

Comprehensive Budget. Synonym of Master Budget.

Compulsory Liquidation. Synonym for a Winding Up by the Court.

Compulsory Winding-up. A winding up other than a Voluntary

Winding-up.

Conceptual Framework. Refers to a set of inter-related concepts, explicit or implicit, underlying the procedures of Financial Accounting.

Concertina Methods of Tariff Reduction. Refers to a procedure of tariff reduction, which involves cutting the higher tariff rates, while leaving lower rates unchanged, so that the gap between tariffs gets diminished.

Condorcet Criterion. Refers to a system of collective choice in which the chosen alternative has been that which defeats all other alternative in a series of pairwise (one to one) contests using majority rule. The procedure has been named after the Marquis Condorcet who discussed it in 1785.

Confidence Interval. In an audit context, a random interval which is having the true value of an audited amount with a chosen probability.

Confirmation. Refers to an audit technique in which the auditor requests third parties (e.g. debtors, banks, employees) or the client to confirm statements made in the accounts or financial statements.

Con-man. Abbreviation for 'confidence-trick man'. Applies to a person who wants to make wealth by fraudulent means after creating unreasonable confidence in his honesty and integrity.

Connected Lending. Loans to companies or persons connected with the institution lending the funds, its managers, director or controllers.

Conservatism. Refers to an accounting convention which, where there is a choice of accounting treatments, chooses the one with the least favourable immediate effect on reported profit and financial position.

Consignment Accounts. Accounts which are recording transactions relating to goods on consignment.

Consistency. Refers to a desirable property of econometric estimators.

A consistent estimator has been one whose mean tends to the true value of the parameter, and whose variance tends to zero as the sample size becomes very large.

Consolidated Financial Statements. Financial statements which are incorporating the financial position, annual results and funds flow of a holding or parent company and its subsidiaries into one set of statements.

Consolidated Fund. Refers to the Exchequer account into which are paid gross tax revenue, less repayments and all other Exchequer receipts not specifically directed elsewhere.

Consolidation of Share Capital. The combination of shares into larger units.

Cotsols. Funded Government securities or stock which the Government need not repay until it wishes. The term has been an abbreviation of 'consolidated annuities'.

Consortium Bank. A type of international bank which is formed by groupings of existing banks usually drawn from different countries. These banks appeared in the 1960s and have now established in several financial centres. They are mainly involved in medium-term lending, frequently to multinational companies; they get the greater part of their funds in the eurocurrency market; but they also arrange 'syndicated' loans (i.e. loans raised among a group of lenders) frequently bringing in lenders outside the consortium members.

Constant Capital. In the Marxian scheme refers to that part of capital which has been represented by the means of production law materials and instruments of labour.

Constant Market Share Demand Curve. The term used for the relation between quantity sold and price which faces the firm if all its competitors exactly match any price change made by this firm.

Constant Purchasing Power Accounting. Refers to a system of Inflation Accounting in which all amounts have been indexed by means of a general index reflecting changes in the purchasing power of money.

Consumer. Refers to any economic agent which is responsible for the act of consuming final goods and services.

Consumer Behaviour, Principles Governing. The generalisations which are made in economic analysis relating to the behaviour of a consumer in distributing a limited personal income amongst an infinite variety of goods and services available.

Consumer Credit. Refers to a loan which is given to the consumer for a short period of time, for the purchase of a specific commodity.

Consumer Demand Theory. Refers to that area of economics which defines testable theories of how consumers behave in response change in variables like price, other prices, income changes and so on.

Consumer Durable. A commodity of reasonably long life, like a refrigerator or piece of furniture; as distinct form, say, food—stuffs.

Consumer Equilibrium. Refers to the situation in which the consumer is able to maximize utility subject to a given budged constraint.

Consumer Goods. Products in the actual form in which they will reach domestic consumers.

Consumer Preference, Theory of. Refers to a theory of consumer preference in which the consumer has been asked if he/she 'perfers' one set of goods to another, or is 'indifferent' between them. The theory has been not concerned with by how much the consumer prefers one set of good to another.

Consumption. Means the act of using goods and services to satisfy current wants. While theroetically precise there have been practical problems in measing consumption. The main problem arises in the treatment of consumer durables.

Consumption Expenditure. Refers to aggregate expenditures on goods and services to satisfy current wants.

Consumption Maintenance. Refers to the maintenance intact of a Standard Stream of future receipts (e.g., dividend payments to shareholders).

Contingencies. Conditions which exist at the balance sheet date the outcomes of which will be confirmed only on the occurrence or non-occurrence of one or more uncertain future events.

Contingency Reserve. Refers to the unallocated reserve for contingencies and other requirements which cannot be quantified.

Contingency Theories of Management Accounting. Refers to the theories of management accounting which argue that accounting systems should fit the organizational context in which they are used.

Continuous Budget. Refers to a budget which is continuously updated, a period (month, quarter) being added at the end at the same time that a period at the beginning is dropped.

Continuously Contemporary Accounting (CoCoA). Refers to a system of accounting, associated with Professor Chambers of the University of Sydney, that defines financial position as the measure of the ability of an enterprise to adapt to a changing environment.

Contra Accounts. Refers to accounts which offset each other. Where two enterprises are both debtors and creditors of each other a complete or partial contra settlement may be made.

Contract. An agreement which is either oral or in writing, whereby one party undertakes to do something for the other party to the contract.

Contract Unit. Refers to the actual amount of a commodity which is designated in a given futures contract.

Contractual Savings Institutions. Institutions like life insurance companies and pension funds, whose schemes and policies have been characterised by regular contributor payments and by defined obligations for future payments in respect of such events as retirement or death.

Contribution. Refers to the excess of revenues over variable costs which is available to cover an enterprise's fixed costs and, if sufficiently large, to provide a profit.

Contribution Income Statement. The term used for an income statement (profit and loss account) which discloses a Contribution Margin and emphasizes the distinction between variable and fixed costs.

Contribution Margin. Sales less all variable costs (whether manufacturing, selling or administrative).

Contribution Margin Ratio. Refers to the total Contribution Margin divided by the total sales.

Contributory. The term used for a person who is liable to contribute to the assets of a company in the event of its being wound up.

Control Account. Refers to an account which contains in summary form the detailed accounts kept in a Subsidiary Ledger.

Controllable Costs. Costs that can be influenced by a given manager within a given time period.

Convenient Social Virtue. Refers to a description by Professor John Kenneth Galbraith of virtues which have been held up as eternally desirable yet serve the ends of the more powerful members of the community. Merit has been ascribed to any pattern of behaviour, however uncomfortable and unnatural for the individual involved, that serves the comfort or well-being of, or has been otherwise advantageous for, the more powerful and influential members of the community.

Convergence Thesis. An idea that socialist and capitalist economies have been departing from their respective 'ideal' forms and are evolving increasingly similar modes of behaviour and thinking, institutions and methods.

Conversion Cost. Refers to the sum of Direct Labour and Factory Overhead, both variable and fixed.

Convertibility. Refer to the freedom to exchange any currency for another currency at the ruling rate of exchange.

Convertible Securities. Refer to the securities which may be converted at given price ratios at the option of the holder at a future date or dates into securities of a different form.

Co-operative Banks. Small local institutions, which are generally organised by a group of individuals with a common bond or purpose.

Co-ownership Firm. Refers to a firm in which control and ownership have been largely in the hands of the employees of that firm.

Co-partnership Industry. Schemes which are introduced by individual firms to provide employees a bigger stake in the prosperity of the firms they work for.

Corporate Capitalism. The term used for a contemporary view of modern developed western economies in which the productive sector has been dominated by large corporations characterized by a separation of ownership from control.

Corporate Modelling. The term used for the construction and use of a computer-based model of an organization to carry out the calculations required to produce results of business activities based on given sets of assumptions and predictions.

Corporate Paper. Notes which are sold by large corporations in the money market as a means of getting funds; such notes are secured by the general credit standing of the corporation.

Corporate Planning. Refers to an approach to top level management problems which emphasises:

(a) the need for an organisation to decide exactly what its objectives are; and

(b) the need for long-term planning in every part of the organisation to achieve these objectives.

Corporate Risk. The total risk involved in a business is termed as corporate risk. It comprises two main types of risk. Financial risk which is arising out of debt finance, and business risk which has been the basic risk involved in the firm's day to day operations.

Corporate State. Refers to an economic and political system where the major sectors of the economy have been organized into single large corporations and administered through the collaboration of government, worker's organizations and organized employer's associations.

Corporation. The term used for a contemporary form of business organisation in the United States of America and elsewhere having two distinct characteristics: it is a legal entity separated from its owners, the stockholders; and it has been usually on a scale much too large for the sole proprietor or partnership to manage or fund.

Corporation Tax. A tax levied on the profits of companies. It is in lieu of income tax and profit tax.

Correspondent Banks. A bank which is acting as agent for another bank in place where the latter is having no office, or for some reason is unable to conduct certain operations for itself.

Cost. Means the amount to expenditure incurred in obtaining the services or a factor of a production.

Cost Accountant. A person employed in an industry to provide a continuous check and control over all forms of expenditure. The method which he employes is known as costing.

Cost Accounting. Refers to the accumulation and assignment of historical costs to units of product and departments, primarily for purposes of stock (inventory) valuation and profit (income) measurement.

Cost Accumulation. Refers to the collection of cost data in an organized way by means of an accounting system.

Cost Behaviour Pattern. Synonym for Cost Function.

Cost-benefit Analysis. Refers to a systematic comparison between the cost of carrying out a service or activity and the value of that service or activity, quantifying, as far as possible, all costs and benefits whether direct or indirect, financial or social.

Cost-benefit Ratio. A ratio calculated:

$$\frac{\text{Gross Benefit (present value)}}{\text{Gross Cost (present value)}}$$

The gross costs and benefits have been discounted over the life of the project by a selected annual rate of interest.

Cost Centre. Refers to the smallest segment of activity or area of responsibility for which costs are accumulated.

Cost Co-efficient. Refers to the cost of a unit of output, e.g., the cost of processing a kilogram of material or the cost of mining a ton of coal.

Cost Control. Refers to the procedure by which the management accountant evaluates the actual cost of a capital project or a manufacturing operation for the purpose of comparison with the authorised estimates or cost standard.

Cost Curve. A graph which shows by means of a curve the expenses which a firm will incur in attaining any given volume of output.

Cost Effectiveness. Refers to the achievement of a particular objective at the least cost. A cost effectiveness approach has been most useful where outcomes cannot easily be quantified in monetary terms whereas costs can be.

Cost-effectiveness Analysis. A technique which is closely related to cost-benefit analysis. Its thus aids choice between options but cannot answer the question whether or not any of the options are worth doing.

Cost Estimation. Refers to the attempted measurement of historical costs.

Cost Flow Assumption. In the context of Inventory Valuation assumptions made about the flow of individual items of inventory (stock) which cannot be physically identified.

Cost-inflations. Refers to a type of inflation, sometimes called cost-push inflation, in which powerful unions have been blamed for making large wage demands in the absence of excess demand in the labour market.

Cost Minimization. For any given level of output that choice of input combination which provides the smallest possible total cost. The choice of a cost minimizing firm facing fixed input prices and using the two factors inputs, Capital K and Labour L, can be illustrated using isocost lines and isoquants.

Cost Function. Refers to the relationship, expressed as an equation between a cost and one or more variables.

Cost of Capital. Refers to the cost which is measured as a percentage rate of the various sources of capital required to finance capital expenditure.

Cost of Sales. All costs which are incurred in a factory in converting raw materials into a finished product: such costs include raw materials, labour, and factory overheads.

Cost of Sales Adjustment (COSA). Refers to an adjustment in Current Cost Accounting (CCA) systems to eliminate Stock Appreciation from reported profit. In principle the adjustment should be made each time a sales takes place in order to base cost of sales on the cost current at the date of consumption instead of at the date of purchase.

Cost of Service Principle. Refers to a basis for charging for services, regard being had to the costs of producing a particular service rather than the value of the service to the consumer.

Cost-plus Pricing. Refers to a pricing practice whereby firms add a margin on to average variable cost so as to cover fixed costs and some reasonable level of profits.

Cost Prediction. The attempted measurement of expected future costs.

Cost-push Inflation. Refers to a sustained rise in the general price level arising from an autonomous rise in costs. This may arise from either an autonomous decision by employees to demand higher real wages or by employers to raise their profit margins or it may arise from an autonomous increase in import prices.

Cost of Production. Expenditure which is incurred by way of payments for rent, mortgages, interest on loans, dividends, salaries and wages, buildings, plant and machinery and raw materials, in the production of a commodity or a service, including development and marketing costs.

Cost Savings. Refer to those Holding Gains that represent the excess of the current cost over the historical cost of inputs used in producing outputs sold.

Countercyclical. Refers to the moving in the opposite direction to a given phase in the trade cycle.

Countervailing Duty. Or matching duty. A situation achieved when an excise duty on an article produced at home becomes equal to the customs duty imposed on a similar article imported from abroad, neither the home produced or imported product being given an advantage.

Coupon Bond. A bond having interest coupons attached to the coupons have been clipped as they become due and have been presented by the owner for the payment of interest.

Coupon Interest Rate. The interest rate attracted by the coupons attached to a bond.

Coupon Rate. Refers to the rate of return on a bond or debenture expressed as a fixed percentage of the face value.

Cournot's Duopoly Model. This model is based upon the behavioural assumption that each of the two firms will maximize profits assuming that its competitor's output remains constant.

Covering. Buying a security previously sold short.

CPP Accounting. Current Purchasing Power (CPP) Accounting.

Craft Unions. Trade Unions which organize all workers having a particular skill, or group of related skills, regardless of the industry in which they work.

Crawling Peg. Refers to a compromise arrangement between a fixed exchange rate and a floating exchange rate, where the exchange value of a currency has been allowed to alter over time but only by some agreed-upon percentage each year.

Creative Accounting. Refers to the use of accounting to mislead rather than help the intended user.

Credentialism. Means the problem of hiring standards that have been too severe for the limited skill requirements of the lower grade jobs in question.

Credit. A wide term which has been used in connection with operations or states involving lending, generally at short-term. To 'give credit' is to finance, directly or indirectly, the expenditures of others against future repayment.

Credit Card. A card which is issued to customers by a bank or group of bodies or other agency (e.g., Diners' Club) which provides the holder direct access to credit, e.g., from a retailer, hotel etc., or, in the case of some cards issued by banks, to cash from the banks operating the particular scheme.

Credit Ceiling. In monetary policy, refers to an announced limit on the amount of credit which may get extended by specified in titutions, usually banks, during restrictive policy phases.

Credit Control. The term which is denoting the set of measures used by the monetary authorities to control the volume of lending by certain groups of financial institutions e.g., bank credit, hire purchase credit.

Credit Creation. Refers to the process by which a group of deposit—taking and lending institutions which are operating on fractional reserve ratios can, on the basis of an increase in their reserve assets, produce an increase in the volume of their lending, and the associated deposit liabilities, of an amount greater than the increase in reserves.

Credit Entry. Refers to an entry in a double—entry bookkeeping system recording an increase in a liability; an owner's equity item or a revenue; or a decrease in an asset or an expense.

Credit Management. Refers to the management of an enterprise's debtors (accounts receivable).

Credit Guarantee. Refers to a type of insurance whereby a credit guarantee association offers insurance against default.

Credit Multiplier. Refers to the ratio of the change in the volume of lending by a group of deposit-taking financial intermediaries (and especially banks) to the change in reserve assets which initiated the change.

Creditor Nation. A nation having a balance of payments surplus.

Credit Rating. Means an evaluation of the soundness of an individual or business firm as a credit risk. It has been usually based on the three 'Cs' of credit:

(a) character or integrity;

(b) capacity, or earning power; and

(c) capital, or the overall financial status of the applicant.

Creditors. Amounts (representing either cash or a claim to services) owed to an accounting entity.

Creditors Ledger. The subsidiary ledger in which creditors' accounts are recorded. Also known as the bought ledger or purchase ledger.

Credit Rationing. The act of rationing loan finance by non—price means in situations of excess demand for credit, by financial intermediaries.

Credit Restrictions. The measures which are taken or imposed by the monetary authorities, to limit or reduce the volume of credit extended by banks and other financial institutions.

Credit Sale. A procedure for purchasing goods under which the purchaser is paying deposit on receipt of the goods followed by a number of instalments until the debt gets cleared.

Credit Sales System. A credit sales system, which may be offered as an alternative to hire-purchase, under which ownership is obtained at the outset. The borrower must, of course, continue to make the agreed payments.

Credit Squeeze. A policy phase of credit restrictions.

Credit Transfer. The system by which funds can get transferred directly through the banking system to the account of a specified recipient. Such a transfer may get initiated simply by anybody, whether a customer or not, paying money into a bank office with the necessary credit slip.

Credit Union. A group of people engaging in organised self-help who are able to save their money together and make low-interest loans to each other. The loans have been usually short-term consumer loans, but may extend to loans for farm or small business enterprise purposes.

Creeping Inflation. A slow, but continuous inflation, which can result inter alia from increases in aggregate demand.

Critical Path Method (CPM). A form of Network Analysis suited to projects where past experience provides a useful guide to the future and the relevant information can be fairly accurately estimated. The activities comprising a project are set out in a network diagram showing the sequence in which each activity can be commenced and its duration. The critical path has been that path through the network that provides the minimum time for the project, obtained by summing the activity times of the path having the longest duration. The only way in which the duration of a project can be shortened has been to reduce the time allotted to activities on the critical path.

Cross. To buy and sell simultaneously in the same contract month for the same commodity.

Cross-elasticity of Demand. The responsiveness of quantity demanded of one good to a change in the price of another good.

Cross-entry. A category used with regard to new entrant firms who are already established firms in industries using similar technology to that in which entry has been taking place.

Cross-section Analysis. The analysis of a series of records of economic data for different groups of people, firms or countries, at the same moment or in broadly the same period of time.

Cum. A Latin word meaning with. Thus: cum dividend, cum rights, etc.

Cum All. With-all advantages. Refers to a description which may get attached to the sale of a security, implying that any dividend interest, rights, bonus or other benefit, just declared or current has been not being withheld.

Cum Bonus. With bonus just declared. Refers to a condition which may get attached to the sale a security.

Cum Interest. With current interest. A condition which may get attached to the sale of a security.

Cum Rights. With 'rights' recently issued. A condition which may get attached to the sale of a security.

Cumulative Preference Share. A preference share which entitles the holder to receive not only the current dividend but also any unpaid arrears, before any dividend has been paid to ordinary shareholders.

Current-deposit Ratio. Refers to the ratio of the public's holdings of currency to its holdings of deposits at banks.

Currency Hedge Market. Refers to a currency market which provides hedging against future currency rates of exchange.

Current Account. An account kept at a bank on which cheques can be drawn and on which interest is not usually paid; also, an account in the books of sole traders and partnerships recording fluctuating amounts of proprietorship interest (i.e., shares of profit less drawings).

Current Assets and Liabilities. Current assets have been those assets of the company which have been reasonably expected to be realised in cash, or sold, or consumed during the normal operating cycle of the business.

Current Cash Equivalent (CCE). The measure of assets and liabilities used in Continuously Contemporary Accounting (CoCoA).

Current Cost Accounting. A system of inflation accounting in which assets have been recorded in the accounts of a company at their 'value to the business', i.e., the loss the business would suffer if the asset get destroyed, in money terms.

Current Cost Depreciation. The depreciation based on current costs rather than historical costs. Current cost depreciation may be based on the cost of a Modern Equivalent Asset or of replacing the services received from the existing asset.

Current Cost of Goods Sold. Cost of Goods Sold in current cost (normally Replacement Cost) terms rather than historical cost.

Current Cost Operating Profit. The conventional accounting profit after making a Cost of Sales Adjustment (COSA), a Depreciation Adjustment and a Monetary working Capital Adjustment (MWCA).

Current Liability. A liability which is expected to have been paid within one year from the date of the balance sheet.

Current Operating Performance Concept. The inclusion in the profit and loss account (income statement) of items relating only to the normal activity of each year; i.e., extraordinary items and prior year adjustments are excluded.

Current Operating Profit. The profit that results from the matching of current revenues from operations with the current cost of those operations.

Current Purchasing Power (CPP) Accounting. A system of Inflation Accounting in which nominal pounds or dollars are replaced by constant pounds or dollars.

Current Ratio. The ratio of current assets to current liabilities. It is a widely used test of liquidity, of a less short—term nature than the Quick Ratio.

Current Value Accounting. A general term which is for accounting systems that take account of changes in Specific Prices rather that changes in the General Price Level and in which assets are valued at current Replacement Cost, Net Realizable value, Net Present Value or some combination thereof.

Customs and Excise. The agency responsible for the assessment and collection of Customs Duties, Excise Duties and Value Added Tax in many countries.

Customs Union. A grouping of countries within which trade restrictions get abolished but which is having a concerted commercial policy towards non-members and a common external tariff on imports from them, though the tariff rate may be varying between commodities.

D

Daisy Chain Schemes. Commercial schemes in which the ownership of a commodity gets transferred through the hands of a chain of subsidiaries, tax-haven companies, affiliates, and other companies, a commodity may be sold at a low price for export and re-imported later for sale at a higher world price, leaving offshore a substantial untaxed make-up.

Damage Cost. The money cost of damage done by pollution. In economics, pollution is generally considered to be an instance of an externality.

Dangling Debit. Refers to a debit balance on Good-will account deducted from shareholders' funds instead of being shown as an asset.

Dated Security. Refers to any security, like a bond, which has a stated redemption date.

Dawn Raid. Refers to a sudden acquisition of substantial shareholdings in a company in circumstances which appear to deny to some shareholders the opportunity of selling their shares at the price offered.

DCF. Abbreviation of Discounted Cash Flow Analysis.

Dear Money. Refers to phases when interest rates have been high compared with their historical average values.

Dear Money Policy. The policy by which loans are made difficult to get. This may be done by raising the interest rate. This policy is used to combat inflation. The opposite policy is cheap money policy.

Death Duties. A general term for taxation of wealth at death, including in particular Estate Duty.

Debentures. A document setting out the terms of conditions of a loan. The debenture holders are to be paid a fixed annual rate of interest. The deberture holders have a first claim on the assets of the company. Debentures are different from shares.

Debenture Discount. The discount which arises from issuing debentures (as in normal) at less than their par value.

Debenture Redemption Reserve. Refers to a Capital Reserve which is set up voluntarily by transfers out of profits. By the date of redemption the amounts transferred should be equal to the redemption value of the debentures.

Debit. In double entry book—keepings, this term is used for entry on the left hand side of an account.

Debit Entry. Refers to an entry in a double-entry book—keeping system recording an increase in an asset or an expense, or decrease in a liability, owner's equity item or revenue.

Debt. Refers to a sum of money, or quantity of goods or services, owed by one individual or body to another.

Debt Finance. It involves borrowing. It refers to the use of loans by companies to finance their operations, especially capital expenditure through long-term loans.

Debtor Nation. A nation having a balance of payments deficit.

Debtors. Amounts which are representing either cash or a claim to services owing to an accounting entity. The Balance Sheet Formats include the following debtors: trade debtors (arising from the sale of a good or service), amounts owed by group and related companies, prepayments and accured income, and called up share capital not paid.

Debtors' Repayment Period. Refers to a measure of the average length of time taken for debtors to pay their accounts.

Decimal Currency. Metallic and paper currency in which each successive denomination is ten times the value of the next below it.

Debtors Ledger. Refers to the subsidiary ledger in which debtors' accounts are recorded. Also known as the sold ledger or sales ledger.

Decision Model. Refers to a method for deciding among courses of action. A formal decision model requires an Objective Function, a set of alternative actions to be considered, a set of probabilities of each state of nature occurring, and a set of outcomes or payoffs.

Decision Table. Refers to a systematic statement in table form of the contemplated actions, states of nature, probabilities and outcomes contained in a Decision Model.

Decision Tree. A diagram which is setting out possible actions, their outcomes and associated probabilities in tree form.

Decreasing Costs, Law of. This law refers to the tendency towards falling average costs of production in taking advantage of the economies of scale, over the long period.

Decreasing Returns. Law of Diminishing Returns, Returns of Scale.

Decreasing Returns to Scale. Refers to a possible response of total output to change in the scale of the production process.

Deed of Transfer. Means a formal agreement under seal bearing a government revenue stamp and signed by both the buyer and the seller of.

Deep Discount Bond (DDB). A bond which is carrying a low or zero interest coupon and issued at a substantial discount. Tax benefits may arise from lack of symmetry in the treatment of borrowers and lenders.

Deferred Charge. An expenditure which is carried forward to be written off in future periods.

Deferred Income. Income which is received or recorded before it is deemed to be earned, a portion of which is transferred annually to the credit of the profit and loss account, the balance being shown in balance sheets as a separate item or under creditors (amounts falling due after more than one year or within one year, according to circumstances).

Deferred Shares. Shares conferring, for example, a right to a fixed percentage divided after all other classes of shares have received a fixed percentage dividend. Such shares are now very rare.

Deferred Taxation. Refers to the taxation attributable to Timing Differences, i.e., to differences between profits as computed for taxation purposes and profits as stated in financial statements.

Deficiency or Surplus Account. An account which is required by law to be attached to a Statement of Affairs.

Deficit. Refers to a situation where outgoings exceed income, on an ongoing basis, or where liabilities exceed assets at a specific point in time.

Deficit Below-out. Means an unexpected and unplanned enlargement of a Government budget deficit due to a combination of unforeseen and unforceable events.

Deficit Financing. Means situation where expenditure exceeds income such that a deficit is operated deliberately. Keynes was the first to suggest that governments should deliberately run a planned deficit as part of monetary policy.

Deficit Units. Means economic units who cannot meet their expenses in a given period from their incomes during that period, either from the sale of their labour, or their assets, such that they have been dependent on borrowing moner or obtaining credit.

Deflation. Means situation in which prices and money incomes have been falling, accompanied by an increase in the value of the monetary units.

Deflationary Gap. Aggregate expenditure runs short of that needed to produce a level of national income which would ensure full-employment.

Deflator. Means an implicit or explicit price index used to distinguish between those changes in the money value of gross national product which is resulted from a change in prices and those which is resulted from a change in physical output.

Deindustrialization. A trend in a national economy towards a larger and larger share of the gross domestic product is taken up by services.

Demand. Refers to the amount of a commodity or service which will be bought at any given price per unit of time.

Demand, Cross-elasticity of. Refers to the responsiveness of the demand for a commodity or service to changes in the prices of other commodities. It is calculated as follows:

$$\frac{\text{Percentage change in demand for commodity X}}{\text{Percentage change in price of commodity Y}}$$

Demand Curve. Means a graphical illustration of a demand schedule or demand function but, given that diagrams can only be drawn in two or three dimensions, showing the relationship between demand and only one or two variables influencing demand, the others being held constant.

Demand Management. Regulating the demands for a good through proper monetary, fiscal and other policies of the government.

Demand Price. Refers to the price which buyers are prepared to pay for a given quantity of a good or service.

Demand Management Policies. Keynesian policies of pursuing an activist, stabilisation course by regulating aggregate demand so as to minimise unemployment and curb inflation.

Demand, Theory of. Refers to a branch of economic theory which deals with analysing the determinants of a consumer's choice of a particular set of goods from all those that are available for purchase especially with how a consumer's tastes and income, and the prices of the goods influence his/her pattern of purchases.

Demonetization. Withdrawing the legal tender status given to a currency, e.g., the demonetisation of 1,000 rupee denominations in 1977.

Demurrage. The penalty payment to be made for delaying a ship or completion of work.

Demurrage Charges. Refers to the monetary penalty which is paid to compensate for the delaying of a ship or freight car due to a consignee's failure to load, unload or sail within an allotted amount of time.

Deposit Banks. Banks whose primary business has been the receipt, transfer and encashment of deposits.

Demand-shift Inflation. Means a theory which is combining elements of demand-pull and cost-push inflation which considers inflation to be a result of a change in the structure of aggregate demand.

Demand-pul Inflation. Refers to a sustained rise in aggregate demand beyond the full employment level of output which results in a sustained rise in the general price level.

Depletion Accounting. Refers to a method of Depreciation appropriate to Wasting Assets in which the cost or other valuation amount of the asset has been apportioned over accounting periods in proportion to the rate of extraction.

Deposit. Sums lent to certain financial institution, e.g. banks, building societies and finance houses, on terms permitting withdrawal with or without notice, or providing for repayment after specified periods—such sums have been described as 'on deposit'.

Deposit Account. A type of account which is designed to attract customers' less active balances, and also as a savings medium.

Deposit Money. Money created by the commercial banks constituting the greater proportion of the supply of money.

Deposit-type Financial Institutions. Institutions which take deposits from the public; they may be bank or non-bank.

Depression. Means prolonged and severe slowing-down of economic activity exemplified by mass unemployment and a level of national income well below its potential level.

Depreciation. Refers to a measure of the wearing out, consumption or other loss of value of a Fixed Asset, arising from use, effluxion of time or Obsolescence.

Depreciation Adjustment. An adjustment in Current Cost Accounting (CCA) systems to eliminate from reported profit the difference between current cost depreciation and historical cost depreciation.

Depreciation Methods. Refer to the methods of allocating the cost or revalued amount (less estimated residual value) of a Fixed Asset systematically over its estimated economic life.

Deprival Value. Synonym for Value to the Business.

Depth Testing. The retracting by an auditor of the chronological sequence of documents related to a transaction.

Devaluation. The reduction in the official rate at which a country's currency is exchanged for foreign currencies. The revised rate is fixed by the government. Indian rupee was officially devalued in 1949 and 1966.

Developed Nations or Industrial Nations. Those countries which have achieved substantial manufacturing and service capability in addition to advanced techniques in agriculture and raw material extraction.

Developing Countries. This description of the poorer nations of the world came into current usage in the 1960s and started to replace the less complimentary expressions 'underdeveloped or 'backward'.

Devise. A gift of realty made by will.

Different Costs for Different Purposes. The philosophy, that a measure of cost is dependent upon the purpose for which it is required.

Differential. Refers to the difference between physical price and futures price.

Differential Cost. Refers to the difference in expected total cost if a given decision is made.

Differential Rate of Interest. Different interest rates for different categories of borrowers.

Dilution. Refers to the decrease in control and Earnings per Share suffered by existing shareholders on a new issue of shares or a conversion of other securities into shares in which they have a less than proportionate share.

Diminishing Marginal Utility. Means the phenomenon whereby it is assumed that the marginal utility attached to an extra unit of any good diminishes as more and more of that good has been purchased.

Diminishing Returns, Law of. Refers to a generalisation that while an increases in some inputs relative to other fixed inputs in a productive process may, in a given state of technology, cause total output to increase there will come a point where the extra output resulting from the same additions of extra inputs has been likely to diminish.

Direct Costs. Costs that can be traced to a finished good in an economically-feasible manner.

Direct Debit System. Refers to a system for periodical payments (both fixed and variable) in which the debit to the purchaser's account is initiated by the seller not the purchaser.

Director's Report. A report to shareholders required by the Companies Acts.

Direct Tax. A tax which is assessed on and collected from those who are intended to bear it.

Dirty Float. Refers to a type of floating exchange rate which is not completely freely floating because central banks interfere from time to time to alter the rate from its free market level.

Disappreciation. Means a movement of prices which, while downward in direction, was merely a correction of a previously excessive rise.

Discount. (a) Refers to a reduction in a previously determined price granted to a customer or class of customers;

(b) Also, refers to the difference between the price at which a security was issued and the price at which it now stands.

Discounted Cash Flow. Refers to the discounting of expected future cash flows to take account of the Time Value of Money.

Discounted Cash Flow Method. Refers to a method of comparing the profitability of alternative projects. This method may be subdivided into:

(a) yield method, and

(b) net present value method. Both of these techniques are using as a measure of the 'rating' of an investment the present cash value of a sum to be received at some future date, discounted at compound interest. The present value or worth of a sum to be received at some future date will be such an amount as will, with compound interest at a prescribed rate, equal the sum to be received in the future. The yield method has been based upon the assumption that the best investment is that from which the proceeds would yield the highest rate of compound interest in equating the present value of the investment with future proceeds. In the net present value method an appropriate percentage rate get stipulated, the present value of the cash inflow is determined using this percentage, the original ccast of the investment is subtracted therefrom, and the resulting surplus is the net present value of the investment.

Discount House. A business institution which will buy acceptances from their owners for less than their face value and hold them to maturity.

Discount Market. Narrowly defined, the market in which treasury and commercial bills are traded.

Discount Yield Formula. A formula which has been used to discount bills of exchange e.g., a bank accepted bill.

Discovery Sampling. In an audit context, a samplıng plan which is designed to control the level of beta risk, i.e., the risk that an auditor will accept a population when he should have rejected it.

Discretionary Costs. Fixed Costs that arise from periodic appropriation decisions.

Disinflation. Refers to the removal of inflationary pressure from the economy so as to maintain the value of the monetary unit.

Diseconomies of Growth. Means the dynamic constraints which set in beyond some high rate of growth and impair the efficiency of the firm's activities. On the supply side, organizational and financial constraints operate.

Disguised Unemployment. Another name for under employment. A person is employed but not to the maximum of his normal ability for want of opportunity,

Seasonal Unemployment: The state of lack of employment opportunities in particular seasons.

Disinflation. Refers to the process of eliminating or reducing inflation.

Disintermediation. Means a process of cutting out the financial middle man, both in short term money markets and long-term (capital) markets.

Disposable Income. Income less tax payments.

Dissaving. Means consumption in excess of current income. Consumption financed out of wealth or out of anticipated future income by borrowing.

Distributed Profits. Refers to that portion of net profits which are released by firms in the form of dividend payments to the owners of equity capital.

Distribution. Branch of economics which deals with the determination of payments made to the factors of production for their share in the work of production, these being known as rent, wages, interest and profits.

Distribution Costs. An expenditure heading required by two of the four Profit and Loss Account Formats.

Dividend. A share of profits paid to share holder of a company Preference dividends have precedence over ordinary dividends. It is not compulsory for a company to pay dividends.

Dividend Control. Limitation of dividend payments by government regulation.

Dividend Cover. Refers to the ratio between Earnings Per Share (EPS) and ordinary dividend per share. It is a measure of the extent to which current dividends are covered by current earnings and may help in forecasting future dividends.

Dividend Growth Model. A model which makes an assumption about the future growth of dividends.

Dividend Policy. Refers to a company's policy on the division of its profits between distribution to shareholders as dividends and retention for investment.

Dividend Reinvestment Plan. Refers to a procedure whereby share holders can automatically reinvest in the same company part or all of the dividends to which they are entitled.

Dividend Washing. Buying a security just after dividends have been paid and selling it just before the next payment so as to avoid tax on income as distinct from capital gains.

Dividend Yield. Refers to the ratio between a company's dividend per ordinary share and the market price per share.

Domestion Credit Expansion. Referred to as DCE. It is an indicator of monetary change within an economy which was developed and strongly advocated by the IMF in the 1960s as a truerd current measure of expansionary forces in the monetary system than measured changes in the money stock.

Donationes Mortis Causa. Gifts which are made in expectation of death and conditional on the subsequent death of the donor.

Dormant Companies. Companies that during any accounting period have had no significant accounting transactions.

Double Counting. Refers to the counting of a single element of benefit or cost more than once in a cost benefit analysis.

Double Declining Balance Method. A declining (reducing) balance method of depreciation used in the U.S.A.

Double Entry. Refers to a system of recording financial events which recognizes that each event has a dual aspect, one of which gives rise to a debit entry, the other to a credit entry.

Drawing. Refers to a method of determining the order in which creditors have to be paid off.

Dual Decision Hypothesis. In modern developments of Keynesian economics, it refers to the argument that conventional demand and supply functions do not offer the relevant signals for equilibrium to come about in markets.

Dual Economy. Refers to a term descriptive of an economy under—going important developments in say both primary and secondary industry.

Dualism, Theory of. This theory was outlined originally by Malthus who saw an economy as having two major sectors, one industrial and one agricultural; breaking the economy into two sectors and looking at the interaction between them has been said to increase the understanding of the development process.

Dual Pricing Policy. The policy of the Government by which the government fixes the statutory price at which a commodity should be made available to consumers by the producers under the control system and another price is allowed to be determined by market mechanism for sale in the open market.

Dumping. A term used in international trade for unloading large quantities of a commodity produced in one country into another at low price. Certain countries resort to dumping to kill competition..

Duopoly. Refers to a market situation in which there have been only two sellers, neither seller being able to ignore the actions and reactions of the other.

Duopsony. Refers to a market situation in which there have been only two buyers of a particular good or service.

Dynamic Economics (or Economic Dynamics). Refers to the inter—temporal analysis of the economic system. The economy may be passing from one equilibrium point to the other, (i.e., two comparative static equilibrium) or it may be continuing through time without reaching a state of Statin equilibrium.

E

Early Warning System. Any technique adopted which gives an early indication of an economic problem likely to lie ahead.

Earmarking. Refers to the practice of linking particular elements of public expenditure to the revenue raised by specific taxes.

Earned Income. For tax purposes, income other than Investments Income.

Earnings. (1) In labour economics, earnings is used to describe the total payments an individual receives from his employment.

(2)The earnings of a business refers to the income of that business which may be either distributed to shareholders or retained.

Earnings Drift. A rise in earnings in excess of the rise in negotiated wage rates.

Earnings Per Share (EPS). The earnings of a company which is attributable to the ordinary shareholders (common stockholders) divided by the number of ordinary shares.

Earnings Yield. Refers to the ratio between a company's Earnings Per Share and the market price per share.

Easy Money. Refers to a general state of case and cheapness of borrowing in the financial system. It may be resulting from policy action to reduce interest rates, increase liquidity of the banking system, relax any non-price restrictions on lending like credit ceilings and restrictive conditions on hire purchase contracts.

Econometric Models. Pioneered by Klein mathematical models which are designed to assist in forecasting the needs and demands of the national economy some years ahead. Models are constructed for static or dynamic economic situations, and the interaction of forces (i.e., the in-built economic assumptions) can be isolated and studied.

Economic Appraisal. Means the study of the economic implications of a project, as a first step in assessing its acceptability.

Economic Base. Refers to those economic activities whose growth and development has been said to determine the economic growth of a town or region.

Economic Base Multiplier. The term used for a form of regional multiplier which is able to estimate the effect of changes in an area's economic base on the economy of the area as a whole.

Economic Development. Refers to the process of improving the standard of living and well being of the population of developing countries by raising per capita income. This is usually realised by an increase in industrialization relative to reliance on the agricultural sector.

Economic Efficiency. Refers to the efficiency with which scarce resources have been used and organised to achieve stipulated economic ends.

Economic Ends. Means the objectives of economic activity. Ends have been both quantitative, and qualitative but with the nature of ends economics has no direct concern, economics deals only with the humber of ends and with their degree of relative intensity.

Economic Friction. Influences, natural or deliberate, which tend to impede the full or rapid operation of economic laws.

Economic Growth. Means the growth per head of the population in the production of goods and services of all kinds which are available to meet final demands.

Economic Indicators. Statistics which are sensitive to changes in the state of industry, trade and commerce.

Economic Interpretation of Theory. A theory which was developed by Karl Marx (1818-1883). This theory asserted:

(a) The forms or conditions of production are the fundamental determinant of social structures which in turn breed attitudes, action and civilizations; and

(b) The forms of production themselves have a logic of their own, that is to say, they change in accordance to necessities inherent in them so as to produce their successors through their own working.

Economic Law. Refers to a statement of what will take place in the economic world under specified conditions. George J. Stigler, in his 'Theory of Price' offers the following statement of an economic law if:

(a) An entrepreneur seeks maximum profits.

(b) His marginal cost curve does not fall so fast as (or more rapidly than) his marginal revenue curve; and

(c) The curves are continuous.

Then he operates at the output where marginal revenue equals marginal cost.

Economic Liberalism. Refers to the doctrine which advocates the greatest possible use of markets and the forces of competition to co-ordinate economic activity.

Economic Man. Refers to the name given to the 'construct' in economics whereby individuals have been assumed to behave as if they maximize utility, subject to a set of constraints of which the most obvious is income.

Economic Nationalism. Usually, a concomitant of political nationalism. It is also a reaction to the frustrations of multinational solutions to common trade problems resulting in unilateral measures for protecting the national interest, most narrowly defined.

Economic Problem. Refers to a problem of ensuring that all available resources have been used to the best possible effect, in the resolving of which decisions must be made as to which ends have to be satisfied first and perhaps which wants will have to get left unsatisfied.

Economic Quantities or Aggregates. The term used for the subject-matter of macro-and micro-economics, economic quantities or aggregates which include such diverse items as the amount of a commodity produced, stored and consumed; the volume of employment and unemployment; the price of butter; the interest on bank loans; the wages of brick-layers; the price of houses; taxes on tobacco or spirits, the surcharge on imported raw materials, etc.

Economic Rent. Refers to a payment to a factor in excess of what has been necessary to keep it at its present occupation.

Economics. A social science which is concerned with how people, either individually or in groups try, to accommodate scarce resources to their wants through the processes of production, substitution and exchange.

Economic Surplus. Refers to the difference between the output of an economy and the necessary costs of producing this output whereby necessary costs have been meant wages, depreciation of capital and the cost of raw materials.

Economic System, Functions of an. Refers to the functions of an economic system which could be defined as follows:

(a) Generally, to match supply to the effective demand for goods and services in an efficient manner;

(b) To determine what goods and services have to be produced and in what quantities;

(c) To distribute scarce resources among the industries producing goods and services;

(d) To distribute the products of industry among members of the community;

(e) To provide for maintenance and expansion of fixed capital investment; and

(f) To fully utilise the resources of society.

Economic Value. Refers to an alternative and rather imprecise term for Net Present Value in the context of Asset Valuation.

Economic Welfare. Defined by A.C. Pigou as that part of social welfare that can be brought directly or indirectly into relation with the measuring rod of money.

Economies of Growth. At or below some rate of growth it can be argued that economies of growth are likely to dominate and provide the growing firm advantages over the stationary one.

Economies of Scale. Refers to the reductions in the average cost of a product in the long run, resulting from an expanded level of output.

Economist. The term used for a social scientist who has become an expert in dealing with the economic aspects of social phenomena. He may specialise in theoretical or applied economics.

Economy. In the context of a Value for Money Audit, the acquisition of resources of an appropriate quality at minimum cost.

The three sactors of the economy:

Primary: Agriculture, forestry, animal husbandry, fishery.

Secondary: Mining and minerals, power generation and fuels, manufacturing industries.

Tertiary: Transport, communication, trade, banking and services.

Effective Annual Rate. The relationship between the interest earned or paid in a year and the principal outstanding at the beginning of the year.

Effective Demand. Demand which is measured by spending on consumption (goods and services more or less used up immediately); on investment (plant, buildings, equipment, stocks), and on the difference between exports (which adds to demand for output at home) and imports (which satisfies home demand without adding to home output.

Effective Rate of Protection. Defined as the increment in value added made possible by the tariff structure as a proportion of the free trade value added.

Efficiency. Maximization of the amount of output per unit of input.

Efficiency Earnings. If economists take of the tendency of competition to equalize earnings in the same local labour market, they are implicity referring to efficiency earnings.

Efficient Market Hypothesis (EMH). Refers to the hypothesis that the stock market is a highly efficient pricing mechanism. Efficiency in this context does not refer to the organizational and operational aspects of the market or to the efficient allocation of resources within the economy but to the capacity of the market to convert information into share prices.

Efficient Portfolio. Refers to a combination of securities which maximizes the expected return on the securities for a given variance (standard deviation) or, equivalently, minimizes risk for a given expected return.

Elasticity. May be defined as a measure of the percentage change in one variable in respect of a percentage change in another variable.

Elasticity of Demand. Generally, refers to the (own) price elasticity of demand, but care should be taken to specify which elasticity of demand is being discussed.

Elasticity of Demand, Income. Refers to the response of the demand for a commodity to changes in the real income of consumers. Its computation has been as follows:

$$\frac{\text{Percentage change in quantity demanded}}{\text{Percentage change in income}}$$

Elasticity of Demand, Price. Refers to the response of demand to a changes in the price of a commodity. It is measured:

$$\frac{\text{Percentage change in quantity demanded}}{\text{Percentage change in price}}$$

Elasticity of Input Substitution. May be defined as a measure of the responsiveness of the optimal labour/capital combination to a change in the relative prices of the two inputs (or the term may be generalized to refer to any two inputs).

Elasticity of Substitution. Refers to a measure of the case of difficulty of substituting between commodities (by consumers) or between factors of production (by producers). The elasticity of commodity substitution may be measured by the following relation:

$$\frac{\text{Percentage change in the ratio in which two commodities are combined}}{\text{Percentage change in the ratio of their marginal utilities}}$$

Elasticity of Supply. Means the response of supply to a change in the price of a commodity. If the price rises, the amount supplied will normally get increased. The elasticity may be calculated as follows:

$$\frac{\text{Percentage change in quantity supplied}}{\text{Percentage change in price}}$$

Electronic Funds Transfer (EFT). Refers to the systems for the transfer of money in which processes based on paper are replaced by electronic techniques.

Eligible Margin. Means the cash or other collateral which a commodity exchange specifies that members may be able to accept from their customers for the purpose of satisfying initial and variation margin requirements.

Eligible Paper. Refers to the financial assets which the central bank is prepared to buy (rediscount) or accept as security for loans, in particular circumstances and usually in dealings with defined institutions.

Embargo. Prohibition of entry of goods from certain countries into a particular country. The embargo is generally imposed by a country to show its disapproval to policies or constrained relations with another country.

Emoluments. Are defined as that portion of management's salary and non—pecuniary benefits which are not part of the entrepreneurial supply price.

Employee Report. A corporate financial report to employees, which is published either separately or as a supplement to a house magazine. Employee reports are often also made available to shareholders and to other interested parties.

Employment, Classical Theory of. It is a theory which is held by the Classical School of economist and based on two fundamental postulates:

(a) The wage will be equal to the marginal product of labour; and

(b) The utility of the wage when a given volume of labour is employed is equal to the marginal disutility of that amount of employment, i.e., the real wage is just sufficient for inducing the volume of labour actually employed to be forthcoming.

Postulate (a) represents the demand schedule for labour, and postulate (b) the supply schedule for labour.

Employment Report. A report, included in a company's annual report, giving details of such matters as numbers of employees, their age and sex distribution, their geographical location, the costs (including pensions and fringe benefits) of employing them training schemes and costs, recognized trade unions, and health and safety measures.

Endogenous Income Hypothesis. A theory which states that utility has been a function of both consumption expenditure and of wealth.

Endogenous Money Supply. Refers to the situation where the level of the money supply will be determined by forces within the economy itself, like rates, of interest, and the level of business activity.

Engel Curve. Refers to a line which plots the relationship between an individual's income and his consumption of a specified good.

Engel's Law. Refers to a generalisation that states that the proportion of income spent on food tends to decline as income grows, with given tastes, or preferences. This law of tendency was postulated by Ernst Engel (1821-96) in a paper published by him in 1857.

Entity View. A view of an enterprise or group of enterprises that stresses the importance of the enterprise itself rather than its owners.

Entrepreneur. The term used for the organizing factor in production. Entrepreneurs have been responsible for such economic decisions as what to produce, how much to produce and what method of production to adopt.

Entry. Refers to the record of a Transaction or other Event in a Journal or a Ledger.

Entry Values. In the context of Asset Valuation, values based on purchase prices in a market either at the date of acquisition (Historical Cost) or at the date of a balance sheet (current Replacement Cost).

Equal Pay. This terms is used to refer to equality between the saxes as regards the terms and conditions of employment.

Equal Sacrifice Theories. In the ability-to-pay theory each taxpayer tries to make the same sacrifice of utility which he gets from his income.

Equlibrium. A term used to describe a situation of economic agents or of aggregates of economic agents such as markets. Applied to an individual agent, such as a consumer or firm, it is used to describe a situation in which the agent is under no pressures or incentives to alter current levels or states of economic action, because given his aspirations and the constrains he faits he to improve his position in term of any economic criteria.

Equilibrium Level of National Income. Refers to that level of national income which exhibits no tendencies to alter. In the simple Keynesian income-expenditure model this would be where the level of injections equalled the level of withdrawals.

Equilibrium Price. Means the price at which a market has been in equilibrium.

Equilibrium Rate of Inflation. Refers to the fully anticipated rate of inflation. Refers to that rate of price inflation at which expectations have been fully realized.

Equi-marginal Returns Law of. A basic theorem which describes the way in which consumers with limited resources divide their expenditure between the innumerable different goods and services they would enjoy, based on the assumptions that consumers wish to get the maximum utility from their income and that they act rationally in seeking the end.

Equities. A synonym for ordinary share (UK) and common stock (USA).

Equity. Another name for ownership; often used to describe a share in a company.

Equity Accounting. Refers to a method of accounting for investments in Associated Companies (broadly companies in which an investor company has a minority ownership but exercises a significant influence) in which credit is taken for a share of profits (or losses) rather than dividends and the investment is carried not at cost but at cost plus a share of undistributed profits (with or without an adjustment for Goodwill). Equity accounting is sometimes known as one-line consolidation.

Equity Capital. It is synonym for Ordinary Shares. Equity Share Capital has a legal definition which includes participating preference shares as well as ordinary shares.

Equity Share Capital. The issued share capital of a company except shares limited to a specified amount as regards dividend and capital.

Equivalent Commodity Scale. Refers to a numerical factor which is applied to the level of consumption of certain commodities by household in different circumstances in order to indicate levels of consumption needed for each type of household to reach a given standard of living.

Equivalent Units. Output expressed in terms not of physical quantities but the amount of resources (materials, labour, overhead) applied. Equivalent units are used mainly in Process Costing.

Escalators. Offer a mechanism for periodic adjustments of wage rates based on movements in a specified price index.

Essentialist Arguments. Arguments in economics which are concerned with correct definitions, labelling, and classification, rather than facts.

Estate Duty. A tax on wealth passing at the time of death.

Estate Economy. A sector or whole economy in an under-developed country which is mainly used for large-scale production of export crops normally managed and owned by foreign powers; it was very prevalent during the colonial era.

Estimation Sampling. In an adult context, estimating the population values of variables (e.g., total sales), or attributes (e.g., the proportion of particular types of sales to total sales) from a sample.

Euro-currencies. The currencies of the European Economic Community together with euro-dollars.

Evening Up. Buying or selling to offset an existing market position.

Event. In an accounting context, a Transaction or other internal or external change recognized by a recording system.

Ex. Without or minus.

Excess Burden of Taxation. A cost which is arising from a tax which is not compensated for by a benefit, this leading to a loss of economic welfare.

Excess Demand. Refers to a state in which demand exceeds supply at some given price. The excess demand curve will slope down wards from left to right and will cut the vertical (price) axis at the equilibrium price.

Excess Supply. Refers to a state in which supply exceeds demand at some given price.

Exchange. Means the act of accepting one thing for another, e.g. as in barter or in a transaction involving money.

Exchange Control. Refers to the system whereby the State exercises control over all or some transactions in foreign currencies and gold, undertaken by its nationals.

Exchange Rate. Refers to the price of a currency in terms of another currency. Exchange rates have been regularly quoted between all major currencies, but frequently one important currency, e.g. the dollar, has been used as a standard in which to express and compare all rates.

Exchequer. The term used for the central account of the central government held by the Treasury at the Central Bank.

Excise Duties. Taxes which are levied on goods manufactured and consumed within a country.

Executor (Executrix). The person who is appointed by a will to administer the estate of a deceased testator.

Executorship Accounts. Accounts which are relating to the estate of a deceased person. The form of accounts a similar to that of Trust Accounts in general.

Executory Contract. A mutually unexecuted contract, i.e., one in which two parties have agreed to make a transfer of resources but neither has yet done so.

Exit Values. In the context of Asset Valuation values which to based on the sale prices in a market at the date of a balance sheet, i.e., Net Realizable Values.

Exogenous. A term which describes anything pre-determined or given in a piece of economic analysis.

Expansionary Phase. Refers to the phase of the trade cycle which will be following a trough or lower turning point, lasting to the next upper turning point or peak.

Export. The term used for a good or service which is produced in one country and sold to and consumed in another.

External Balance. The balance in a country's international payments.

External Economy. Refers to a fall in the cost of any of the materials and services which a firm requires, which are obtained from outside source.

Externalities. Benefits and costs which have been not received or borne by the enterprise responsible for them and hence do not usually appear in their accounting records.

F

Face Value. The value stated on the face of goods. This is to be differentiated from its market rate.

Factor Cost. Refers to the price net of indirect taxes and subsidies. It is being the amount received by the factors of production during the manufacture of a good.

Factor Incomes. Incomes accuring to the factors of production which are wages, salaries, profits, interest and rent.

Factoring. Refers to the sale by an enterprise of its debts to a factor who not only collects the debts but may also provide administrative and book-keeping services and credit insurance facilities.

Factor Markets. Refer to the markets in which factors of production or inputs have been bought and sold, e.g., the labour market, the capital market.

Factor-price Differentials. Refers to the situation where a factor of production is having two separate prices; for example, the price of labour between capitalistic wage-based production and family based production activities.

Factor-price Frontier. The term used for the name assigned by Paul Samuelson to the negatively sloped trade off between the wage rate and the rate of profit in growth theory.

Factors of Production. The term used for the resources of society which are used in the process of production. These have been usually divided into three main groups land, labour, capital, but may also include entrepreneurship.

Factory Burden. Synonym for Factory Overhead.

Factory Overhead. All costs which are associated with a

manufacturing process other than direct materials and direct labour.

False Trading . Refers to the trading at dis-equilibrium prices.

Feedback. In an accounting context, information about performance which is furnished to the persons responsible for that performance.

Fellow Subsidiaries. Refer to the companies that are subsidiaries of the same company but not of each other.

Feudalisms. The terms ascribed to a type of political and economic system which had been dominant in Europe in the Middle Ages. It get characterized by a social pyramid extending from the dependent peasant through the 'fief' endowed lords and knights to the monarch.

Fiat Money. Money which the State declares to be legal tender, although its content value may be little or nothing.

Fiduciary Issue. That part of the bank note issue of the Reserve Bank of India, that is backed by the government and the other securities and not by gold. The fiduciary issue is regulated by Parliament by law.

Filtering. A term which has been used in urban economics to describe a process by which housing changes in quality, generally passing from occupation by higher income groups to occupation by lower income groups.

Finance. Narrowly interpreted it means capital in monetary form, that is in the form of funds lent or borrowed, normally for capital purposes, through financial markets or institutions.

Finance Act. The term used for an Act of the Parliament imposing and changing central government taxes. There is at least one Finance Act each year.

Finance Bill. A bill not involving goods, simply promising to pay a specified sum of money on a specified date.

Finance Commission. Under the Constitution of India, a Finance

Commission is to be constituted every fifth year or at such earlier time as the President consider necessary to make recommendations to him as to:

(i) the distribution between the union and the states of the net proceeds of taxes which are to be or may be divided between them under the Constitution and the allocation between the states of the respective shares of such proceeds;

(ii) the principles which should govern the grants-in-aid of the revenues of the states in need of such assistance from the Consolidated Fund of India; and

(iii) any other matter referred to the Commission by the President in the interest of sound finance. The recommendations of the Commission together with an explanatory memorandum as to the action taken thereon are laid before each House of Parliament.

Finance Corporations. Refer to the specialised financial institutions which are established to provide medium and long-term finance where it cannot be provided easily from traditional sources.

Finance House. A financial institution which is engaged in the provision of hire purchase and other forms of instalment credit. Also known as finance companies, hire purchase finance houses, and industrial banks.

Finance Lease. Sometimes termed as a 'full payout lease', a contract between lessor and lessee for the hire of a specific asset selected from a manufacturer or vendor of such assets by the lessee.

Financial Accounting. Refers to that part of accounting which is concerned mainly which external reporting to shareholders, government and other users of accounting outside the enterprise.

Financial Budget. Refers to that part of the Master Budget of an organization which is concerned with such matters as cash and capital expenditures, and pro forma balance sheets and funds statements.

Finance Failure. A term which includes both economic failure.

Financial Futures Contract. The term used for a futures contract for a financial instruments which commits the seller to deliver and the buyer to take delivery of it at the contracted price.

Financial Institutions. Private or governmental organisations which carry out the vital function of facilitating the flow of savings from those businesses and households with surplus funds to businesses and households with insufficient funds to meet immediate needs, or carry out a central role in the supply of money and credit.

Financial Instrument. Refers to any document which is an evidence of debt, and the sale or transfer of which makes the seller to acquire finance.

Financial Intermediaries. Refers to persons and institutions who collect funds and invest them on behalf of others, e.g., unit trusts, investment trusts, pension funds.

Financial Mathematics. Refers to the mathematics of Compound Interest and Annuities.

Financial Modelling. Refers to that part of Corporate Modelling which is concerned with the construction and use of computer-based models to carry out the calculations necessary to produce financial statements based on given sets of assumptions and predictions.

Financial Planning. Refers to that part of long-range planning concerned with the financial aspects of company's objectives, and strategies for meeting those objectives.

Financial Planning Models. Refers to the mathematical statements of the relationships among all the operating and financial activities of an organization, account being taken of relevant outside factors. Financial planning models are usually computer-based.

Financial Ratio. Refers to the relationships among items in financial statements. They are normally expressed in either ratio form, e.g., current assets / current liabilities = 2.0

or in percentage form (e.g., current liabilities are 50% of current assets).

Financial Risk. Risk which results from an increase in Gearing (Leverage).

Financial Statements and Budget Report. A summary of the central government accounts published annually by the government.

Financial Statements. Refers to the statements which are giving financial information about an accounting entity. The traditional financial statements and the Balance Sheet and the Profit and Loss Account (income statement).

Financial Structure. Synonym for Capital Structure.

Financial Year. Different bodies employ different financial years for financial accounting and this need not be coincident with the standard calender year.

Fine Tuning. The term refers to government policies which aim to make small changes in taxation or expenditures which in turn have been designed to influence employment levels, national income and price levels.

Finest Rate of Discount. Lowest rate of discount.

Firm. Refers to a unit of management which is operating under a trade name organised either to extract minerals, produce or manufacture goods, or to sell goods or services, or to engage in two or three of these activities simultaneously.

First In First Out (FIFO). In the context of Inventory Valuation, this term refers to the calculation of the cost of inventories (stock and work in progress) on the basis that the quantities in hand represent those most recently purchased or produced.

First Mortgage Bond. A fixed interest loan repayable on a given date; similar to debenture. The term 'first mortgage' implies that the bond holders have a claim before other creditors on the assets of the corporation.

Fisc. Refers to the persons and institutions who are responsible in any country for the assessment and collection of taxes.

Fiscal Drag. The term used for the action of a progressive tax system in taking an increasing portion of the national incomes as nominal incomes rise over time.

Fiscal Dividend. Refers to the increase in federal or national revenues which results from a rise in the Gross National Product at any given level of tax rates.

Fiscal Illusion. Refers to a situation in which the benefits of particular government expenditure have been clearly identified by recipients but the costs are not, being widely dispersed over time and population.

Fiscalists. Refer to those who believe that fiscal policy has been the most important means available to the government for influencing the level of economic activity.

Fiscal Multiplier. Refers to a coefficient that indicates by how much an increase in fiscal expenditure influences the equilibrium level of income.

Fiscal Policy. Generally refers to the use of taxation and government expenditure for regulating the aggregate level of economic activity.

Fiscal Year. US term for what is usually called Financial Year in the UK and India where fiscal year refers to the tex year.

Fisher Effect. The hypothesis, named after the economist Irving Fisher, that the nominal rate of interest embodies in it an inflation premium sufficient, on a one-for-one basis, to compensate lenders for the associated with inflation.

Fisher's Ideal Index. An index which has been based on a formula devised by the American economist Irving Fisher (1867-1947). It is intended to be a 'true' index, the Laspeyres' index giving an upper limit and the Paasche index a lower limit to this 'true' index, it is in fact an index of the geometric mean of the Laspeyres and Paasche indices. The formula has been as follows:

$$\left[\frac{\Sigma P_n q_o}{\Sigma P_o q_o} \times \frac{\Sigma P_n q_n}{\Sigma P_o q_n} \right]$$

where P_o= price in the base year; q_o= quantity in the base-year; P_n= price in the year being considered, and q_n= quantity in the year being considered.

Fixed Assets. Assets that are intended for use on a continuing basis in an enterprise's activities.

Fixed Charge. A charge which has been attached to some specific asset or assets.

Fixed Cost. A cost which remains unchanged for a given time period and over a Relevant Range of activity.

Fixed Exchange Rates. Exchange rates among national currencies which have been fixed by governments, and have been not free to vary in response to market forces.

Fixed Instalment Method. A method which is used for calculating and allowing for the depreciation of an asset. The fixed instalment, or straight-line, method distributes the cost of an asset uniformly over its depreciable life. The amount to be set a side each year may be calculated from the formula:

$$\frac{P - L}{n}$$

where P represents the initial asset cost, L the expected salvage value at the end of the useful life of the asset and in the plant life expressed in years.

Fixed Interest Securities. Debentures and kindred securities issued by a public company, being known by a variety of names, e.g., mortgage debentures, secured debentures, secured notes.

Fixed Investment. All final goods purchased by firms other than those additions to inventories which have been not intended for eventual resale.

Flat Rate. A rate of interest which is applied to the original sum in a contract rather than to the reducing balance, and therefore potentially misleading.

Flat Yield. Refers to a yield which does not take account of the Redemption value of an investment.

Flexible Budget. Refers to a Budget that is adjusted for changes in volume over a Relevant Range of activity.

Flexible Exchange Rate. Refer the exchange rates among national currencies which have been free to vary in response to market forces, without government attempts to maintain a fixed exchange rate at which one currency gets exchanged for another.

Flight From Cash. Refers to moving wealth from cash into interest bearing assets; either because of expectations of price increases or a fall in the interest rate.

Floating Assets. Obsolete term for Current Assets.

Floating Charge. Refers to a charge which is not attached to any specific asset but to all assets or to a class of assets (e.g., stock and work in progress).

Floating Debt. Refers to that part of the National Debt which involves short-term borrowing: it consists of Ways and Means Advances and Treasury Bills.

Floating Exchange Rate. Refers to a market situation in which the exchange rate between currencies has been free to change from day-to-day in response to supply and demand, the opposite to fixed parity.

Floating of a currency. When the exchange value of a currency is not firmly fixed with reference to any other currency of the world, that currency is said to be floating.

Flotation Costs. The costs which are arising from an issue on a stock exchange of shares or other securities.

Flow. Refers to the quantity of an economic variable measured over a period of time.

Flow of Funds. In the economy, it refers to the transfer of money between the different sectors; the money inflows and out flows by 'transaction group'.

Flow of Funds Accounts. In the context of National Accounting, accounts showing both financial and non-financial flows through the sectors of an economy.

FOB. Free on Board. Term used of goods shipped where the price is not including shipping or insurance charges; opposite to C.I.F. An F.O.B quotation implies that the exporter will deliver the goods free on board a ship in accordance with the contract at the port named; he pays all expenses up to that point.

Folio. The name (derived from the Italian foglio) which is used by accountants to denote a page of a Journal or Ledger.

F.O.Q. Free on quay. Refers to quotation term where goods have to be delivered to a quay, but the loading expenses have to be borne separately by the buyer.

Forced Saving. Refers to a form of saving which takes place because consumers are not able to spend their money on desired consumption goods simply because those goods are not available.

Forecast Reporting. The reporting of projected data to external users of financial statements.

Foreign Aid. Refers to assistance which it given by wealthier countries to aid the less fortunate, often being funnelled through the World Bank and other multilateral development banks.

Foreign Currency Translation. Refers to the restatement of accounts or transactions in one currency into another currency.

Foreign Exchange. Currency or interest-bearing bonds of another country.

Foreign Exchange Market. Means the international market in which currencies are transferred between countries.

Foreign exchange reserves. The total claim of a country on other countries of the world held in the form of foreign currency assets and interest-bearing bonds. Sometimes, the value of gold and SDRS also is included in the calculation of total reserves.

Foreign Exchange Risk. Refers to the risk of loss from carrying out operations, or holding assets and liabilities, in a foreign currency.

Foreign Exchange Transaction. An accounting transaction which is involving a currency other than that in which an enterprise's accounts are kept.

Foreign Investment. Refers to any investment in another country which is carried out by private companies or individuals as opposed to government aid.

Foreign Payments. Refers to any payment that has to be made to a foreign country whether in return for goods and services or as repayment of debt.

Foreign Trade Multiplier. Means the net effect on a country's foreign trade following an increase in spending at home after taking into consideration:

(a) the additional spending on imports to serve the increase in home demand, and

(b) the effect of the increase in imports on the income of the exporting countries and the influence this increase in income may possess on the demand for the exports of the country concerned.

Forex Markets. Foreign exchange markets including forward foreign exchange markets.

Forfeited Shares. The shares forfeited, in accordance with a company's Articles of Association, for non-payment of Calls.

Forward Contract. Refers to a futures contract to buy or sell a specific physical commodity at some time in the future.

Forward Exchange Contract. An agreement to exchange different currencies at a specified future date and at a specified rate.

Forward Exchange Market. The term used for a market in which currencies are bought and sold at rates of exchange fixed now, for delivery at specified dates in the future.

Forward Linkage. Refers to the relationship between an industry or firm and other industries or firms which employ its output as an input.

Forward Market. Any transaction involving a contract to buy or sell commodities, or securities at a fixed future date at a price agreed in the contract, has been part of a forward market.

Forward Rate. Means the rate of exchange at which a currency may be bought or sold for future delivery, on the forward market.

Forward (or Future) Rate Agreement. Interest rate hedging an agreement between a bank and its customer on the terms of a national deposit or loan to begin on a future date.

F.O.T. Free of tax.

Founder's Shares. Synonym for Deferred Shares.

Fractional Reserve Banking. Refers to the practice by which commercial banks maintain a reserve of highly liquid assets equal to some fraction, normally a small one, of their total asset portfolios.

Franchise. 1. Refers to an authorisation or permit to sell products in a particular area;

2. A most important yet least tangible element in the make-up of a successful corporation or bank, the perceived ability in the mind of the client to deliver top-quality services.

Free Exchange Rates. Refers to the exchanges rates which depend upon the supply and demand for a currency on the foreign exchange market, without official intervention.

Free Good. A good, the supply of which has been at least equal to the demand at zero price.

Free Market. Refers to a market in which there is an absence of intervention by government and where the forces of supply and demand are permitted to operate freely.

Free on Board. FOB.

Free Port. A port in which no customs duties are levied for imports or exports.

Free Riders. Users of Public Goods who do not pay for them but cannot be easily excluded from consuming them.

Free Trade. Refers to the trade which is unimpeded by tariffs, import and export quotas and other devices which obstruct the free movement of goods and services between countries.

Free Trade Area. Refers to a loose grouping of countries within which tariffs and other barriers to trade has been removed, while each member country has been its own commercial policy to countries outside the area.

Freight. The amount of payment made by a person chartering a ship or rail wagon for transport of his goods.

Fringe Benefits. All those non-wage and salary elements in the total pecuniary rewards an employee receives from his employment.

Front End Loading. 1. Refers to a characteristic of loan repayments during periods of inflation: high repayments in real terms get incurred in the early years, with lower repayments in real terms towards the end. This front end loading increases as the inflation rate rise.

2.Often termed as a service fee, cost of an investor of buying into a unit trust or purchasing other securities.

Frustration Hypothesis. A hypothesis which states that the higher the actual rate of growth of real income relative to the long run expectations of the workforce, the lower will be the sense of frustration and the less likely the workforce will push for higher money-wages.

Full Cost. The sum of average variable cost, average fixed cost and the net profit margin. It is a concept which is used with reference to firm pricing rules.

Full Cost Pricing. Basing prices on the full costs of products, i.e., on product costs based on Absorption Costing and Normal Volumes, plus a mark-up.

Full-employment Budget Surplus. Refers to a measure of the thrust of fiscal policy which is not relying solely on the magnitude of the budget surplus.

Full-employment Surplus (Deficit). Refers to the surplus or deficit which would take place in a federal or national government budget if the economy was functioning with full (or high) employment.

Full-employment National Income. (Also known as potential national income and national real output). Refers to a measure of the real value of the goods and services that can be produced when the country's factors of production have been fully employed.

'Full Line Forcing'. Refers to a situation in which a company will not supply certain types of goods or machinery (in which it may have an important monopoly) to dealers who do not order also certain other specified types of good or machinery which the company manufacturers.

Functional Fixation. Refers to the tendency of a person to attach a certain meaning to a title or an object and his or her inability to perceive other possible meanings or uses.

Fund. In public sector accounting a separate pool of monetary and other resources established to support specified activities. The fund is an accounting entity and is operated and accounted for independently of other funds.

Funds Statements. Statements that show the sources and applications of funds of an enterprise for a period.

Funded Debt. Refers to that part of government debt which does not have contracted redemption date.

Funding. The conversion of short-term debts into long-term debts, The sale of long-dated securities by the monetary authorities.

Fungible Assets. Refers to the assets that are substantially indistinguishable from one another, e.g., some stocks (inventories) and investments.

Futures. A term used to designate all standard contracts covering transactions in financial instruments or physical commodities for future delivery on an exchange.

Future Costs. Costs which are based on expectations of the future. Future costs, not past costs, have been relevant in decision-making, although the latter often form the basis for prediction.

Future Options. An option in a contract that gives a buyer the right, but not the obligation, to buy something at a sated price within a certain time.

Futures Price. The price of a given commodity unit which is determined by open outcry on a futures exchange.

G

GAB. Abbreviation of General Arrangements to Borrow.

Gains From Trade. Means the increase in welfare to the world economy as a whole or to an individuai country, depending on the viewpoint, because of engaging in international trade.

Gain on Borrowing. Refers to a gain that results from repaying a loan in monetary units of a lower purchasing power (either of commodities in general or of specific commodities) than those at the date of borrowing.

Galloping Inflation. It is the name given to rapid growing inflation, such as that which characterised Germany and several other European countries just after the First World War, when prices rose so rapidly that money quickly lost its value, people lost confidence in the monetary system, and ultimately the system broke down and people resorted to the system of barter. In recent years, the increase in the price of petroleum and allied products by oil producing countries has caused a galloping inflation round the word.

Game Theory. The term used for the theory of making the best choice from among available strategies given imperfect information.

GATT. Abbreviation of General Agreement on Tariffs and Trade.

G.A.T.T. Anti-dumping Code. A code which was introduced by the General Agreement of Tariffs and Trade setting out the criteria for the investigation of complaints of alleged dumping and the imposition of appropriate remedies.

Gearing (Leverage). Refers to the relationship between the funds provided to a company by its ordinary shareholders and the long term sources of funds carrying a fixed interest charge or dividend.

Gearing (Leverage) Ratios. Refer to the ratios which are based on either balance sheet or income data measuring the degree of a company's gearing (leverage).

G.E.M.M. Abbreviation of a gilt-edged market maker. It is a company functioning as a primary dealer in the gilt-edged market.

General Agreement on Tariffs and Trade (G.A.T.T.). An international commercial treaty which came into force on 1 January 1948. Some 88 governments, accounting for over 80 per cent of world trade, had by 1982 become contracting members of the Agreement. Two-thirds of the membership is made up of developing countries. The basic principle of G.A.T.T. enshrined in Article 1 of the Agreement is that trade should not be discriminatory; what applies to one partner should apply to all.

General Equilibrium. The term used for a theoretical situation when supply equals demand in all market-in an economy.

General Ledger. The Ledger having those accounts not contained in the Subsidiary Ledgers.

General Mortgage Bond. Refers to a bond which has been secured by a blanket mortgage on a company's property.

General Price Level Accounting. Synonym for Current Purchasing Power (CPP) Accounting.

General Purchasing Power Accounting. Synonym for Current Purchasing Power (CPP) Accounting.

General Purpose Financial Statements. Financial statements which are prepared for all potential users rather than just one user.

Geographic Frontier. Refers to a term which is used in the theory of economic development to describe an area in which with the existing population, level of technical ability and tastes and preferences, there will occur increasing returns to labour and capital.

Gifts Inter Vivos. Gifts which are made between living persons.

Gibrat's Law of Proportionate Growth. Due to R. Gibrat this is a formulation which is describing how a process of random growth can produce a lognormal distribution of firm sizes. Specifically, the law assumes that the number of firms has been fixed, the distribution of growth rates confronting each firm has been identical, and has been therefore independent of both firms' absolute size and past growth history.

Giffen Good. Means a good whose demand tends to fall as its price falls, thus apparently contradicting the law of demand.

GIGO. Garbage in, garbage out. An expression used (especially in a computing context) to emphasize the fact that the reliability of outputs (e.g., financial statements) depends upon the reliability of inputs (e.g., accounting data).

Gilt-edged. Refers to a high-grade bond issued by a company which has demonstrated its ability to earn a comfortable profit over a period of years and pay its bondholders their interest without interruption.

Gilt-edged Securities. Securities or investments in which the risk is minimum i.e., the repayment of capital interest are certain. Generally applied to government securities.

Global Marketing. Refers to marketing in which all markets have been served which provide scope for sales, there being no rigid distinction in though between home and export markets.

Goal Congruence. Co-ordination of the personal and group goals of subordinates and superiors with those of the organization of which they are a part.

Gold bricking. Refers to the restriction of output by workers under incentive payment system so as to avoid the introduction of higher effort standards per unit of payment.

'Golden Age' Growth. In growth theory it refers to a situation of balanced growth in which the warranted rate of growth will be equal to the natural rate of growth at full employment.

Golden Handshake. Refers to a non-negotiable award given to a top executive whose services are being dispensed with.

Golden Parachute. Means a financial compensation package which is designed and negotiated by top executives prior to any threat of displacement or takeover.

Golden Rule. Refers to the optimal growth path which provides the maximum sustainable level of consumption per person in an economy.

Gold Exchange Standard. Means a variant form of the gold standard under which a country pegged the value of its currency to the value of the currency of a centre country, e.g., sterling, which was itself on gold.

Gold Market. Refers to the market in which metallic gold, coin or bullion, is being traded. There are gold markets in all the main financial centres.

Gold Points. Refer to those exchange rate levels at which, when a currency is on a gold standard, it becomes profitable to buy gold from the central bank and export it (the 'gold export point') or import gold and sell it to central bank (the 'gold import point').

Gold Standard. Refers to a monetary system in which each unit of currency is worth a fixed amount of gold. The rules of a gold standard have been:

(a) all paper currency must be convertible at its face value into gold;

(b) there must be no restrictions on the import or report of gold; and

(c) a gold reserve must be maintained, fully sufficient to meet all demands made upon it.

Goodhart's Law. A law which states that any measure on the money supply that is officially controlled promptly loses its meaning.

Goodness of Fit. Refers to the extent to which an estimated equation

fits the data. It may be measured by the Coefficient of Determination.

Goods. Tangible commodities which contribute positively to economic welfare. To be distinguished from bads.

Goodwill. The goodwill earned by a concern because of his proper working and fair transactions established over a long period. When a concern changes hands, payment is made for transfer of goodwill.

Goods-based Classification of Industries. Basic goods, capital goods, intermediate goods, and consumer goods industries.

Goodwill on Consolidation. Refers to Goodwill which arises on a Business Combination when Acquisition Accounting as distinct from Merger Accounting is used.

Government Securities. A general term which is used for marketable debt of the Central Government, from the shortest term, i.e. Treasury bills, to very long term and undated debt.

Gradualism. Means an approach to economic development policy which indicates that the development process is a slow, steady, gradually increasing phenomenon and that the necessary policy measures should also be of this nature.

Grant. Refers to the funds which are provided by some agency or individual to other agencies or individuals which do not from part of some exchange but represent a one-way transfer payment.

Gratuity. A payment made a person when specific legal obligations for the service rendered by the person.

Gravity Model. This is commonly used approach to certain problems in Regional Economics and transport studies. It represents the amount of interaction between two places as being determined by the size or importance of the places and the distance between them. One such form of interaction has been population movement. Others would be car travel or air travel.

Green Currency. The term used for agricultural unit of account for the European Economic Community. An accounting device only, the exchange rates between the national currency and the unit of account have been called green monies'.

Green Money. Refers to a set of special exchange rates which are used to convert common farm prices into national currencies, in the European Economic Community.

Green Pound. Means the exchange rate for the pound sterling which is used for converting agricultural prices agreed under the Common Agricultural Policy in terms of the European unit of Account into domestic UK prices.

Green Revolution. A term applicable to an increase to the major increase in agricultural productivity obtained in developing countries by the introduction of high-yielding, disease resistent seeds. It is applicable to rice and wheat in particular.

Gresham's Law. A 'law' which was formulated by Sir Thomas Gresham (1519-79), an English businessman and public servant. This theory is able to predict that where two monetary media circulate together, then if their intrinsic relative values as determined by market forces diverge from their legally determined values, the money of higher intrinsic value will be withdrawn from circulation and hoarded.

Gross Cash Flow. Equal to company profit plus depreciation. It does not measure the actual flow of funds in an organisation as it does not take into consideration the movements in assets and liabilities or capital raisings.

Gross Domestic Fixed Capital Formation. Investment in fixed assets, e.g. expenditure on buildings, vehicles, plant and machinery for replacing or adding to the stock of existing fixed assets, expenditure on maintenance and repairs being excluded.

Gross Domestic Product (GDP). The measure of the total flow of goods and services produced by the economy of a country in a year.

Gross Domestic Product at Constant Prices. Refers to the Gross Domestic Product at Factors Cost or the Gross Domestic

Product at Market Prices (taken over a series of years and adjusted to discount changes in the value of money.

Gross Domestic Product at Factor Cost. Means the value of goods and services produced within the nation, representing only the sum of the incomes of the factors of production.

Gross Domestic Product at Market Prices. Refers to the value of goods and services which are produced within the nation, charged at ruling prices. Prices include all taxes on expenditure, subsides being regarded as negative taxes.

Gross Income. As distinguished from Net Income gross income of a firm implies the total income earned by it before taxes and overheads.

Gross Interest. Distinguished from Net Interest, gross interest is one which is calculated with due consideration to extra income earned from the use of money so borrowed.

Gross Investment. Refers to the total investment that takes place in the economy within any specific time period. It comprises replacement investment and net investment.

Gross Margin. Refers to the excess of sales over the cost of goods sold (i.e., for a manufacturing company using Absorption Costing, all manufacturing costs, both fixed and variable, relating to goods sold).

Gross National Product (GNP). Refers to a measure of the production of the goods and services of an economy shown in National Income and Expenditure Accounts. It can be obtained by recording incomes, expenditures or outputs.

Gross National Product Deflator. Refers to a price index which is used to correct the money value to all the goods and services entering Gross National Product for price changes.

Gross Trading Profit. Profit which are earned on operations before allowing for depreciation and interest on debt finance and stock appreciation.

Group Companies. Companies that are subsidiaries or holding companies of other companies.

Group of Seventy-seven. Means a group of less developed countries (actually over 100) who banded together in 1964 to press for better terms of trade with the richer countries. The group has played an important role in international trade and tariff negotiations.

Growth Pole. Refers to a group or cluster of industries which are centered on and linked with one or more propulsive industries and form a centre of growth and dynamism in an economy. The concept was introduced by the French economist Perroux.

Growth-profitability Function. Refers to the maximum profit rate which a firm can sustain at different rates of growth.

Growth Theory. Refers to a part economics which deals with the analysis of the determinants of the rate at which economies growth over time.

Growth-valuation Function. This function provides the maximum valuation ratio a firm can sustain at different rates of growth and is a common features of growth theories of the firm. Reflecting the growth-profitability relationship this function has been likely to be bell-shaped.

Guaranteed Bond (U.S.). A bond which has interest or principal, or both, guaranteed by a company other than the issuer.

H

Hammer Price. Means a price which is calculated according to the rules of the Stock Exchange. It represents the market value of a security at the time of the default of a member firm.

Hard Currency. Means a currency which is having a continuing high level of demand, relative to supply in the market for foreign exchange.

Harmonization. Refers to the process of increasing the compatibility of accounting practices by setting bounds to their degree of variation.

Harrod-domar Model. It is being a synthesis of the independent work of two economists, Sir Roy Harrod (b. 1900) and Evsey D. Domar (1914). The model comprises:

(a) firms which produce and sell goods, spend on new investment, and pay incomes to households for productive services; and

(b) household which spend part of the income they receive on consumption goods and save the rest.

Heckscher-ohlin Law. A principle which was first put forward by Eli F. Heckscher (1879-1952) in 1919, and subsequently refined by Bertil Ohlin (b. 1899). This principle states that advantages in international trade arise from the different relative factor endowments of the countries trading. A country will tend to export those commodities which intensively embody the factor with which it has been most well-endowed.

Hedge. Refers to an action taken by a buyer or seller to protect his business or assets against a change in prices.

Hedger. Refers to one who deals in a physical commodity and who uses futures contracts to manage his price risk.

Hedging. Refers to a technique of insurance against fluctuations in the prices of raw materials or goods scheduled for future delivery by dealing in 'futures'.

Hedonic Price. Refers to the implicit or shadow price of a characteristic of a commodity. The quantity of a particular commodity could be resolved into a number of constituent characteristics which determine its quality.

Heterogeneous Capital. Refers to physical capital of different types which are highly specific to certain production processes and not transferable to alternative processes.

Heteroscedasticity. Refers to an econometric problem in which the variance of the error term in a regression equation does not remain constant between observations.

Heuristics. Simplified rules which are used for processing information on a rule of thumb, trial and error basis.

Hicksian Income Concepts. Concepts of income put forward by the economist J.R. Hicks in his book Value and Capital (2nd ed. 1946). His three ex ante concepts are:

1. 'the maximum amount which can be spent during a period if there is to be an expectation of maintaining intact the capital value of prospective receipts (in money term)';
2. 'the maximum amount the individual can spend this week, and still expect to be able to spend the same amount in each ensuing week';
3. 'the maximum amount of money which the individual can spend this week, and still expect to be able to spend the same amount in real terms in each ensuing week'.

Hicks Neutral Technical Progress. Means a classification of disembodied technical progress which compares points in the growth process at which the capital to labour ratio has been constant.

Highlights. Brief summaries of financial and operating data, especially those included in Annual Reports to shareholders.

High-powered Money. Money consisting of currency (notes and coin) and bank's deposits at the central bank of a country. Part of the currency is held by the public, the remaining currency being held by banks as vault cash. Also called the monetary base; the terms have been interchangeable.

High Seas. That part of the seas or oceans which are outside the territorial waters or exclusive economic zone of different countries.

Hire Purchase. The scheme which facilitates purchase of goods through hire. Since the purchaser is unable to pay the seller price in lumpsum, he is allowed to hire the goods and to pay the sale price along with rent in instalments.

Hire Purchase and Instalment Sale Accounting. Accounting for Hire Purchase and Instalment Sales in the books of finance companies, dealers and purchasers.

Historical Cost Accounting. Refers to a system of accounting which is based on Historical Costs but modified in practice by Prudence (as, for example, in the valuation of stocks or inventories at the lower of cost or market) and, by revaluations of fixed assets.

Hire Purchaser Finance Houses. Finance houses which deal with the granting of credit for the purchase of certain classes of goods on the condition that their advances will be repaid by regular instalments over a fairly short period of time, together with interest charged on the amount borrowed.

Historical Costs. Means the charge incurred at the time a factor input or resource was originally purchased and which will be not thus equal to the cost of replacing the input (replacement cost) if prices rise in the meantime.

Historical Models. Economic models which have been capable of analysing changes and situations in the real world as opposed to equilibrium models which have been largely theoretical.

Hoarding. Refers to the act of holding money. If the desire to hoard increases the result will be (assuming that no new money is created) that money incomes will fall. Conversely, if there is occurs a fall in the desire to hold money, incomes will rise.

Holding a Call. Buying a call option.

Holding a Put. Buying a put option.

Holding an Option. Buying an option.

Holding Company. A company may be a subsidiary of another company if the other company controles the composition of its Board of Directors or if the other company holds more than half of its equity share capital. The parent company is known as the holding company.

Holding Gain. Refers to a gain that results from holding assets rather than using them in operations.

Homemade Gearing (Leverage). Refers to the Gearing (Leverage) of investors as distinct from the gearing of the company in which they have invested.

Horizontal Equity. Refers to the tax principle that equal people in equal circumstances should be treated in an equal way.

Horizontal Integration. Horizontal Integration is said to take place if two firms at the same stage of the production process merge to form a single business organization.

Hotchput. Refers to the bringing into account of any Advancement made to a child during the parent's lifetime. At the death of the testator such advances will, if brought into hotchpot, form part of the estate to be distributed.

Hot Money. Refers to money which gets transferred rapidly from one financial centre to another to take advantage of differences in short term interest rates or to escape the financial penalties of devaluation.

Human Assets. The wealth which is tied up in human beings, including the investment in time and money spent to allow individuals to acquire education, training and skills.

Human Capital. Refers to those investments which are made in human resources so as to improve their productivity.

Human Information Processing. The ways in which decision—makers make use of information under uncertainty.

Human Resource Accounting (HRA). Accounting for the human resources of an enterprise that are excluded from conventional financial statements except insofar as they are included under Goodwill.

Hyper-inflation. Refers to an extremely high rate of increase in the General Price Level.

Hypothecation. Similar to markets. The loanee hypothecates the goods borrowed from a bank or lender as the security for his repayment.

I

IBRD. Abbreviation of International Bank for Reconstruction and Development.

Idle Money. As inactive money that does not contribute to productive effort in an economy.

Idle Time. Wages paid for unproductive time caused by, for example, machine breakdowns, shortages of material or inefficient scheduling.

IMF. An abbreviation of International Monetary Fund.

Imitative Growth. Refers to an aspect of firm growth by diversification.

Immiserizing Growth. Refers to the possible but improbable case where an increase in economic output within a country results via repercussions through trade to a situation where its economic welfare gets diminished.

Impact of Taxation. Means the person, company or transaction on which a tax is levied.

Imperfect Competition. 1. Refers to any form of market structure other than perfect competition and would thus include monopolistic competition, oligopoly, and monopoly.

2. Refers to any market structure other than perfect competition and monopoly.

Imperfect Market. Means a market in which the following conditions, necessary for a perfect market, do not hold good:

1. A homogeneous product;

2. A large number of buyers and sellers;

3. There exists freedom of entry and exit for buyers and sellers;

4. All buyers and sellers possess perfect information and foresight with respect to the current and future array of prices.
5. In relation to the aggregate volume of transactions the sales or purchases of each market agent have been insignificant;
6. There exists no collusion amongst buyers and sellers;
7. Consumers maximize total utility and sellers maximize total profits; and
8. The commodity is transferable. If any one of conditions (1) to (8) are not fulfilled a market has been to some degree imperfect market.

Imperialism. According to Marxist or socialist though, it refers to a foreign policy which seeks political and economic control over backward areas to guarantee the home country an outlet for idle savings and surplus manufactured goods in exchange for strategic raw materials.

Implicit Costs. Mean the costs in the form of lost opportunities to use resources, including time, in another way, e.g., a major implicit costs of a university education has been the foregone opportunity to work and receive an income.

Implicit Price Deflator. A price index which is used to deflate the various spending series that comprise the gross national product.

Implicit Rental Value. Refers to the price the owner of a physical factor of production like capital should charge the firm for the use of that factor.

Implementation Lag. Refers to the time taken to implement monetary policy.

Import. Refers to a good or service which has been consumed in one country but bought from another country.

Import Duties. The taxes which are leveid by the state on imported goods. Besides being a source of revenue these are used for giving protection to domestic industries and for conserving foreign exchange.

Imported Inflation. Refers to price rises due to the increased cost of imported raw materials and goods.

Import Licence. A Government licence required for goods imported into a country.

Import Restrictions. Refer to the restrictions on the quantity or types of goods imported into a country, through the use of tariffs or quotas.

Import Substitution. Finding substitutes to articles whose import should be avoided.

Imputation System. Refers to a system of taxation of companies and shareholders which attempts to avoid the double taxation of distributed profits.

Inactive Money. Refers to that portion of total stock of money or money supply in existence at any one time which is not utilised to finance current transactions or being lent out on the money market.

Incidence of Tax. Refers to the way in which the burden of tax eventually falls, as distinct the apparent burden.

Income. Refers to the wealth, measured in money, which has been at the disposal of an individual or a community, per year or other unit of time.

Income and Expenditure Statement/Account. Refers to a financial statement and ledger account which is prepared by bodies whose major objective is other than making profits.

Income Bonds and Debentures. Bonds and debentures or debenture stock, the interest on which is only payable out of profits.

Income Differentials. Refers to the difference in income levels between different people. These can occur due to types of job, i.e. skill differentials or geographical location in that some areas have higher wage levels than others, or there may be differences between urban and rural wages levels.

Income Effects. Refers to the effect which a change in price of a good or service has on a consumer's demand for the good or service, taking into account the change it induces in his real income.

Income Elasticity of Demand. Refers to a measure of the responsiveness of the quantity demanded of any good to a change in the level of income of the persons demanding the good.

Income Expenditure Model. It is a simple Keynesian one sector model. It shows the determination of the equilibrium level of national income. Under the assumptions of a fixed capital stock, labour force and technology and rigid wages and prices and, therefore, expectations, it describes the static equilibrium in which the supply of real national output is equal to the quantity of national output people wish to buy.

Income in Kind. Income in the form of goods and services rather than cash. Income in kind has been more difficult to tax adequately and fairly than income in cash.

Income Maintenance. Refers to policies which are designed to raise the income levels of specific groups or individuals.

Income-Sales Ratio. Refers to the ratio of a firm's or industry's value-added to total sales revenue. This ratio can be regarded to be a measure of the extent of vertical integration, the greater the integration the higher the index.

Income Statement. A term for Profit and Loss Account.

Income Tax. A Direct Tax on income, as distinct from capital.

Income Tax, Progressive. Refers to a system of graded tax payment, individuals with small incomes paying a smaller proportion of their incomes than individuals with large incomes.

Income Velocity of Circulation. Refers to the measure of the velocity of circulation of money which arises from the Combridge analysis in which average cash balances get related to the level of income in a given period. The equation is M=kPY where M denotes the quantity of money, P represents the price level, Y stands for real income and k for the fraction of nominal income held as cash balances.

Incomplete Records. Refers to the accounting records that are incomplete in some way and fall short of a full double entry system. A business may, for example, record only transactions affecting cash and persons.

Increasing Returns, Laws of. Refers to a generalisation that in many industrial processes a doubling of inputs may give rise to an output that is more than doubled.

Incremental Budget. Refers to a Negotiated Static Budget that takes the previous year's budget and actual results as the starting point, the budget amounts then being changed in accordance with the experience of the previous period and expectations for the period under consideration.

Incremental Cost. Synonym for Differential Cost.

Indemnity. An agreement where by one person agrees to make good any loss suffered by a party to a contract in which he is not himself personally involved.

Independence (of the Auditor). The term used for the ability of an auditor to act with integrity and objectivity, both as an individual practitioner and as a member of a profession.

Independent Project. The term used for a capital investment project the acceptance or rejection of which has no effect on any other capital project.

Indexation. Refers to the adjustment of the terms of contracts by a price index in order to allow for inflation. Contracts are thus fixed in real rather than money terms.

Index Number. A single number which gives the average value of a set of related items, and stated as a percentage of their average value at some base period.

The index number for a particular year can be determined by using the following formula:

$$\frac{\text{Price of selected commodities in the particular Year} \times 100}{\text{(prices of selected commodities in the base year)}}$$

The average of the Index number of both years i.e., the base year and the particular year:

$$\frac{\text{Total Index Number of the year}}{\text{Total number of selected commodities}}$$

Indifference Curve. A curve which is showing the combinations of two goods (including, for example, expected return and risk measured by standard deviation) for which an individual is indifferent.

Indirect Costs. Costs that cannot be traced to a finished good in an economically feasible manner.

Indirect Labour. Labour that cannot be identified with a manufactured good or traced to it in an economically feasible manner.

Indirect Manufacturing Costs. Synonym for Factory Overhead.

Indirect Tax. Refers to a tax that is not assessed on and collected from those who are intended to bear it. Examples are value added tax, sales tax, payroll tax and exercise duties.

Individualism. Refers to the name given to a political and economic system that favours the development of the individual rather than that of the state or other association. It has been the antithesis of collectivism and socialism.

Industrial Bank. An alternative name for a finance house. An organization which provides hire purchase credit.

Industrialization (in developing countries). Refers to the development of industries as a general development strategy.

Industrial Unions. Mean trade Unions which are able to organize all workers within a given industry regardless of the jobs they perform.

Industrial Wages Structure. Refers to the ranking of the average pay levels of different groups of workers which are classified according to the industry in which they are employed.

Industry. Refers to all the manifold activities of a country which offer employment, but more narrowly those activities concerned with the production of goods rather than services.

Inelastic Demand. A change demand is not always proportionate to the change in price. A small change in price may lead to a greater change in demand. In such cases the demand is called elastic or sensitive.

Inertia Selling. Refers to a practice in which goods have been sent to householders without having been ordered.

Infant Industry. Means a young and growing industry.

Inferior Goods. Goods of which less have been bought by people in higher-income groups because they all able to afford to consume more expensive commodities. Inferior goods possess negative income elasticities.

Inflation. The economic situation in a country, of steadily rising prices, resulting in the diminution of purchasing power of money. Excessive amount of inflation is called galloping inflation of hyper-inflation Cost-push inflation is caused by rise in the cost of production, especially because of wage increases. Demand-pull inflation is caused by excessive increase in money supply without a maching increase in production.

Stagflation. The situation in which stagnation and inflation exist side by side.

Recession. Reduction in production and employment over a short period for want of sufficient demand for goods.

Depression. That State of economy in which men and machinery remain idle over a long period for want of sufficient demand.

Deflation. A reduction in the level of economic activity in the economy as a result of failing prices-appreciation in the value of money.

Disinflationary measure. Step taken by the government to bring down prices when inflation is chronic.

Reflation. The State of recovery from recession or depression, caused by introduction of spending measures by the government.

Information Asymmetry. Refers to a situation in which some users of financial statements have superior information to others.

Inflationary Spiral. Refers to an upward trend of prices, which has been partly the result and partly the cause of increases in wages and salaries and other incomes such as profits, dividends, interest and rent.

Inflation Demand-pull. Refers to excessive demand for goods and services, the symptoms of which have been rising prices and scarcities of labour and materials.

Inflation Accounting. Refers to techniques for dealing with the impact of inflation on accounts and accounting procedures.

Inflationary Gap. Aggregate expenditure exceeds the maximum attainable level of output with the result that there occurs upward pressure on prices. In the simple income-expenditure model this is shown by an aggregate expenditure function which cuts the 45^0, where E = Y, beyond the full employment level, Y_f At Y_f the resources of capital and labour have been fully employed with the result that this represents the maximum attainable level of output.

Inflation Tax. Refers to the situation where a government adopts a policy of promoting inflation in place of an increase in taxation to pay for its expenditures.

Informal Sector. Refers to self-employed in a developing country who are engaged in small-scale labour-intensive work like tailoring food preparation, trading, shoe-repairing, etc.

Information Agreement. It is also known as an open price agreement or price reporting agreement. It is an agreement whereby a number of firms undertake to inform each other regularly about past, current and sometimes future prices, and other relevant data like costs, discounts, rebates, conditions of sale, turnover and often the names of buyers.

Information Intermediaries. Persons and institutions who are engaged in the gathering, processing, analysing and interpreting of financial information on behalf of others.

Infrastructure of an Economy. Refers to the underlying capital of a society involving basic amenities for economic development in the country like roads and rail transportation, communication systems, water supplies, electric power, and other public utilities.

Initial Margin. Refers to the deposit which a user of futures markets must make on purchasing or selling a contract.

Injections. Refers to an exogeneous addition to the income of firms or households. An addition to the income of domestic house holds or firms that does not result from the immediate expenditure of the private sector.

Inland Bill. A bill which is drawn for the finance of domestic production or trade.

Innovations. Often used to cover both technological advances in production processes as well as the introduction of different attributes and attribute combinations in marketable products.

Input-output Analysis. Means the quantitative analysis of inter—industry relations. All transactions that involve the sale of products or services within an economy during a given period have been arranged in a square indicating simultaneously the sectors making, and the sectors receiving, delivery.

Inside Money. Forms of money which have been based on private sector debt, the prime modern example being commercial bank deposits to the extent that they have been matched by bank lending to private sector borrowers.

Insider Dealing. Refers to the use of information not publicity available to acquire shares at less than their 'real worth'.

Insolvency. Refers to inability of a debtor (whether an individual or a corporate body) to pay debts as they fall due. Insolvency is a question of fact, not of law.

Instalment Credit. The term used for finance lent on conditions which offer repayment of the principal, together with the interest by regular instalments.

Instalment Sale. Refers to a credit sale in which payments are made by instalments.

Institutional Economics. Refers to a type of economic analysis which emphasizes the role of social, political and economic organizations in dertermining economic events.

Instalment Sale. Refers to a credit sale in which payments are made by instalments.

Institutional Investors. The term used for the shareholders other than persons, industrial and commercial companies, the public sector and the overseas sector, i.e., financial institutions such as insurance companies and pension funds.

Insurance. Refers to the elimination of risk of loss by the payment of premiums to an insurance company which undertakes to pay for specified losses. The losses of the few have been thus met from the premiums of the many. Insurance services are divided into the following classes:

(a) fire, and other hazards such as riots, explosion, earthquake and hurricane;

(b) accident, including motor, third party liability and personal;

(c) marine, both hull and cargo;

(d) aviation, both hull and cargo;

(e) life and endowment; and

(f) cover against default by a borrower. This category includes, credit insurance, mortgage insurance, and financial guarantees.

Insurance Broker. Brokers acting on behalf of the insured.

Intangibles. Costs or benefits which either cannot be quantified, or at least cannot be priced.

Intangible Assets. Assets such as Goodwill, Patents, Trade Marks and Copyrights which have no tangible form.

Integrated Economy. A term which refers to a situation when different sectors of an economy, usually the agricultural and industrial sectors, work together efficiently, and have been mutually interdependent.

Integrated Test Facility. Refers to a computer audit test in which the auditor integrates into the operating system a test person, department or activity so as to determine whether the computer processes the information in the way prescribed.

Intended Inventory Investment. Refers to the deliberate build-up of stocks. The deliberate run-down of stocks has been intended inventory disinvestment.

Intensive Margin. Refers to the case of decreasing physical returns to capital or labour applied to a fixed quantity of land.

Inter-company Profits. Refers to the profits which are earned by one company at the expense of another company in the same group because Transfer Prices are set higher than cost.

Inter-company Transactions. Transactions between the member companies of a group. They are eliminated or otherwise adjusted for during the preparation of Consolidated Financial Statements.

Interest. The reward for the use of capital in the processes of production. The term 'interest' generally means gross interest. Net profit refers to the payment for the use of capital when there is no risk of non-payment or trouble to management.

Interest Cover. The number of times the fixed interest payments made by a company to service its loan capital get exceeded by earnings.

Intergovernmental Grants. Refers to the funds which are provided by one level of government in a country to another level of government.

Interim Dividend. A dividend which is paid or proposed to be paid in the course of a financial year.

Interim Financial Statements. Refer to financial statements which are issued for a period shorter than the normal statutory year, e.g., half-yearly, quarterly.

Interlocking Directorates. The term used for a situation in which one or more person(s) sit on the board of directors of two or more companies.

Intermediate Good. A good which finds use at some point in the production process of other goods, rather than final consumption. Common examples include steel and wood.

Intermediate Lag. Refers to a part of the operational lag which is associated with monetary policy.

Internal Audit. Refers to an element of the Internal Control system set up by the management of an enterprise in order to review accounting, financial and other operations and to determine whether prescribed policies are being adhered to.

Internal Balance. Means a situation in which full employment and price stability are simultaneously achieved.

Internal Check. Refers to that aspect of Internal Control which is exclusively concerned with the prevention and early detection of errors and fraud.

Internal Control. Refers to the whole system of controls, financial and otherwise, established by management in order to carry on the business of an enterprise in an orderly and efficient manner, ensure adherence to management policies, safeguard the assets, and secure as far as possible the completeness and accuracy of the records.

Internal Drain. Means a movement of cash, i.e., circulating media, from the banks into domestic circulation.

Internal Finance. Means those funds which are retained from net profits for use in financing a firm's activities.

Internal Growth. Refers to that part of a firm's expansion which has been produced by investment within the firm rather than investment in acquisition of other firms and merger activity, i.e., external growth.

Internal Rate of Return (IRR). Refers to the discount rate that equates the present value of the expected cash outflows of an investment with the present value of the expected inflows, i.e., it is the rate r, such that

$$\sum_{t=0}^{n} \frac{A_t}{(I+r)^t} = 0$$

where A_t is the cash flow (in or out) for period t and n is the number of periods. It is one of the Discounted Cash Flow methods of Capital Investment Appraisal.

Internally Generated Fund. Trading profits before depreciation and after interest, tax and dividends.

International Bank for Reconstruction and Development (I.B.R.D.). Bank set up under the Bretton Woods Agreement in December, 1945, for two purpose; to help finance the rebuilding of war—devastated areas and to aid in the advancement of less developed countries.

International Development Association (I.D.A). An affiliate of the International Bank for Reconstruction and Development. It was formed in 1960 to help developing nations by extending financial aid on easy terms I.D.A. finances carefully studied and well prepared projects. It will help countries whose credit standing has not enabled them to borrow from the Bank.

International Economics. Deals with that part of economics which is concerned with transactions between countries in the fields of goods and services, financial flows and factor movements.

International Firm. A firm which is undertaking operations on are international basis, without the ownership being on an international basis.

International Gold Pool. An organisation established in 1961 by a number of central banks to operate in the London market for the purpose of stabilising the price of gold. The participating countries had been the United States of America, Belgium, Italy, Netherlands, Switzerland, Western Germany and the United Kingdom. France was also a member but ceased to take an active part in the pool from July, 1967, onwards.

International Liquidity. The term used for the ability of countries to meet their international transactions. Countries keep reserves of gold and foreign currencies and settle their indebtedness to other countries by using either a transfer of gold or payments in their own or foreign currencies.

International Monetarism. Refers to a school of thought which holds that changes in the world money supply have been principal source of inflationary and deflationary pressure in the International economy.

International Monetary Fund. It is an international financial institution which was set up in December 1945, because of the Bretton. Woods Agreement of the previous year. It is an association of governments designed to:

(a) Promote international monetary cooperation through a permanent institution;

(b) Facilitate the expansion and balanced growth of international trade;

(c) Promote exchange stability maintain orderly exchange arrangements among members, and avoid competitive exchange depreciation;

(d) Assist in the establishment of a multilateral system of payments in respect of current transactions between members; and

(e) Provide members with an opportunity to correct maladjustments in their balance of payments without resorting to measures destructive of national and international prosperity.

International Payments System. A general term referring to the way in which international financial transactions have been carried out i.e., payments between residents of different countries who hold different domestic currencies.

International Price Arbitrage. Means the mechanism by which domestic prices get influenced by world prices.

International Trade. The term used for the trade which is carried out between nations in goods and services.

International Trade Theory. A body of economic theory which is relating to international trade, including the following:

(a) the theory of comparative advantage which states that mutually advantageous trade will always be possible with trade patterns based on relative prices, rater than absolute prices; no one country can have a comparative advantage in all commodities;

(b) the Heckscher-Ohlin theory which states that a country will tend to export the commodity that uses relatively more of the factor of production that is relatively abundant in that country;

(c) the factor-price equalisation theory which states that under free international trade, not only the prices of the traded products but also the prices of the factors of production (inputs) such as land, labour, and capital will be equalised among countries.

Intestate. Refers to a person who dies without leaving a Will.

Inventory Accounting. Accounting for Inventories (Stocks). The amount of inventory significantly affects for many enterprises both the Cost of Goods Sold (and hence the gross and net profits) and the Current Asset total in the balance sheet.

Inventory Control. Discovering and maintaining the optimum level of investment in inventories (stocks). The main problem of inventory control is balancing ordering costs (which decline in total as stocks increase) against carrying costs (which increase as stocks increase), in order to calculate the Economic Order Quantity (EOQ) which minimizes total costs.

Inventory-led Recovery. Descriptive of a recovery from an economic recession which starts with the rebuilding of depleted business stocks or inventories.

Inventory Valuation. The methods of valuing inventories (Stocks) either under Historical Cost Accounting (HCA) or under some form of inflation accounting.

Investment Bank. A bank which advises corporations and governments on how to raise capital; guarantees the sale of new bonds and shares, and distributes them to investing institutions and individuals.

Investment Centre. Refers to a segment of a business that is held responsible for investments as well as revenues and costs.

Investment Grants. Refers to a grant of cash by a government to an enterprise in order to encourage the enterprise to purchase fixed assets of a particular kind or in a particular location.

Investment Income. For tax purposes, income from dividends and interest. Some investment income is tax-free.

Investments. Refers to shares, loans, bonds and debentures held either as a Fixed Asset, i.e. to provide a continuing source of income and in some cases control or significant influence over the activities of another enterprise, or as a Current Asset, i.e., as a temporary means of earning income on funds eventually intended for other use.

Investment Trust. Refers to a company whose object is investment in the securities of there companies.

Iron Law of Wages. The hypothesis which states regardless of the possibility of upward movements in wages in the short run wages would inevitably return to the subsistence level in the long run.

Islamic Development Bank. A regional development bank which was formed 1974 by the Organization of the Islamic Conference to encourage economic growth in Muslim countries and communities.

Iso-cost Curve. A curve of line which shows the combinations of any two inputs and can be bought with a fixed sum of money.

Iso-profit Curves. Refer to the locus of combination of two or more independent variables of the profit function which yield an equal profit. It has been a commonly used concept in oligopoly theory.

Issue. Any of a company's securities; or the act of distributing such securities.

Issue by Tender. The term used for an issue of securities in which the public is invited to apply at or above a certain minimum price.

Issued Capital. Refers to that part of the authorised capital of a company which has been subscribed. Such capital will be fully-paid-up, or partly-paid up.

Issued Share Capital. Refers to the nominal amount of the Authorized Share Capital which has been issued.

Issue Price. Refers to the price at which a share, bond or debenture is issued. It is not necessarily equal to the Par Value since shares can be issued at a premium and bonds and debentures at a premium of a discount.

Issuing House. Refers to an institution that advises on new issues of shares of stocks for public limited companies.

J

Jawbone. Descriptive of verbal appeals as an aspect of the voluntary approach to the implementation of monetary policy.

J. Curve. In the period immediately following a depreciation or devaluation of its currency a country may experience a balance of payments deficit. In the subsequent period however this will get eliminated and the current account slowly get moved into surplus. The J. curve is so called because it describes the shape of the time path the current account figures may follow if time has been plotted on the horizontal axis and the balance of trade on the vertical.

Jelly Capital. The term used to refers to that capital when it is theoretically assumed that the capital-labour ratio can get altered immediately.

Job Costing. Refers to a costing system which is used by organizations whose products or services are easily identified by individual units or batches, each of which receives varying inputs of direct materials, direct labour and factory overhead.

Joint Costs. Refers to the costs of two or more products of relatively significant sales value that are simultaneously produced by a process or series of processes.

Joint Product. Refers to a product of a relatively significant sales value that can only be produced simultaneously with other products.

Joint Profit Maximization. Means the maximization of the combined profits of an existing group of firms.

Joint Profits. Means the profits which are earned by a small group of rival firms.

Joint Sector. That sector in an economy in which public and private Sectors collaborate.

Joint Stock Banks. The banks whose stocks are jointly held by the public and private investors. These banks are of two categories: (i) scheduled and (ii) non—scheduled.

Joint Variance. A Variance which is reflecting the combined effect of changes in prices and quantities.

Joint Venture. Refers to the joint prosecution of a particular transaction for mutual profit or an association of persons jointly undertaking some commercial enterprise.

Juglar Cycle. Business cycles of between 9 and 11 year's duration which were identified by Clement Juglar of France. Juglar divided business cycles into three phases: prosperity, crisis and liquidation. He argued that the sole cause of the crisis had been the prosperity phase that preceded it, and that depression always followed the crisis; the excesses and maladjustments of the prosperity phase made the crisis and depression inevitable. Standard business cycle theory deals mainly with explanations of the Juglar cycle. These theories have been classified by Gottfried Haberler as: purely monetary theories, monetary overinvestment theories, nonmonetary overinvestment theories, underconsumption theories, and psychological theories. Most modern theories have been based on time lags occurring in necessary adjustments between production and demand, investment and interest rates, and so on.

Journal. Refers to any book (or other record) in which either one or both aspects of an accounting Transaction of other event are recorded chronologically on a day-to-day basis.

Judgemental Sampling. In an audit context, sampling which is based on the exercise of an auditor's judgement rather than on statistical techniques.

Kabutocho. Tokyo's equivalent of Wall Street.

Kaffirs. South African mining shares.

Key Bargain. Refers to a specific form of wage leadership in which a single pay settlement acts as a point of reference for all subsequent wage claims.

Keynes Effect. Refers to a change in the demand for commodities because of a change in the general price level.

Keynesian Economics. A term which is used to describe macro—economic theories of the level of economic activity using the techniques developed by J.M. Keynes.

Keynesian School. A school of economists which in whole or substantial part supports the following tents:

(a) Fiscal policy has a greater influence in the economy than monetary policy, i.e., money supply is regarded to have a negligible effect on output and prices—'money does not matter';

(b) an incomes policy is important in helping to achieve an inflation rate limitation;

(c) it is possible to obtain a more stable macro—economic environment if policy instruments are used in a discretionary manner by the authorities rather than being set according to some simple rules;

(d) exchange rates have been an important policy instrument in achieving a balance-of-payments target;

(e) tax rates (and to a lesser extent government expenditure) may get adjusted so as to keep unemployment at a reasonable level, ensure low inflation, and achieve a balance-of-payments equilibrium.

Kinked Demand Curve. It is a demand curve which may be characteristic of firms in certain oligopolistic industries; it occurs when a firm judges that if it cuts its prices, other firms will cut theirs too; but that if it raises tis prices, other firms may be content to leave theirs unchanged (in this event a potential loss of market is involved). Thus, the demand curve has been relatively inelastic below the going price, and relatively elastic above the going price.

Kite. A bill, often called 'accommodation bill' drawn on a person who has received nothing in return.

L

Labour. All human resources which are available to society for use in the process of production.

Labour Variances. Refer to the deviations from budget or standard costs in respect of direct labour. They are generally subdivided into rate or Price Variances and Efficiency Variances.

Labour-costs Per Unit of Output. Refers to the cost of the labour in real terms which is involved in making each unit output from a factory.

Labour Economics. Deals with the study of the nature and determinants of pay and employment.

Labour Intensive Industry. Refers to an industry in which the ratio of labour input to capital input has been higher than the average ratio for industry as a whole.

Labour Market. Concerns the activities of hiring and supplying certain labour to undertake certain jobs, and the process of determining how much shall be paid to whom in performing what tasks.

Labour Power. A term which is used by Karl Marx to describe the commodity which workers sell to capitalists.

Labour-Saving Techniques. Refers to a technological process or production method which has been biased towards mechanization and sparing use of manpower.

Labour's Share. The share of wages in the national income. There are two competing theories of labour's share; the marginal productivity theory and the neo-keynesian theory.

Labour Supply. Or supply of effort, the total number of hours of work that a population has been willing to supply.

Labour Theory of Value. A theory which is employed by the classical economists, e.g., Ricardo and especially Marx, to explain the determination of relative prices on the basis of quantities of labour, immediate and accumulated, embodied in goods.

Labour Turnover. Means the number of workers who leave, or are replaced, in a given period. It is expressed as a percentage of the average number of workers employed during the period.

Lapping. The US term for Teeming and Lading.

Laissez-faire. Refers to a policy of non-interference by the State in economic affairs. The underlying philosophy is that man is moved predominantly by self-interest and that there exist certain immutable laws which produce a natural harmony.

Land Tax. A tax which is based on the land values or size of land holdings.

Last in First Out. In the context of Inventory Valuation, the calculation of the cost of inventories (stocks) on the basis that the quantities in hand represent the earliest units purchased or produced.

Law of Demand. The widely accepted view that, other, things being equal, more of a good will be bought the lower is its price, and the less will be bought the higher is its price.

Law of Diminishing Returns. This law states that when increasing quantities of a variable factor get added to fixed quantities of some other factor, first the marginal and then the average returns to the variable factor will, after some point, get diminished.

Law of Supply. This law may be stated that other things remaining the same, changes in supply are caused by changes in price. If price goes up, supply rises and it falls if there is a fall in price.

Law of Variable Proportion. The law of variable proportions states that "If one factor of production is fixed while another factor of production (variabie) is increased, average and marginal products will rise, reach a maximum and then decline".

Learning Curve. Refers to a Cost Function in which Average Costs decline systematically as cumulative production increases.

Lease. The term used for an agreement in which one agent obtains the use of some property owned by another agent for a given period of time in return for an agreed fixed charge which is generally paid in periodic instalments.

Lease Accounting. Refers to accounting for contracts between a lessor and a lessee for the hire of a specific asset, the lessor retaining ownership of the asset but conveying the right to the use of the asset to the lessee for an agreed period of time in return for payment of specified rentals.

Ledger. A book or other record which is having Accounts. In practice a business of any size will subdivide its ledger into a General or Nominal Ledger and several Subsidiary Ledgers.

Legacy. Refers to a gift of Personalty made by a will. Legacies are either 'general' (a gift out of the general funds of an estate), 'demonstrative' (a gift payable out of a particular fund or portion of an estate).

Legal tender. This currency (coins and bank notes) which have to be accepted in payments.

Lerner Index. Refers to an indicator of monopoly power which is defined as:

$$\frac{\text{price-marginal cost}}{\text{price}}$$

If prefect competition exists, price equals marginal cost; therefore the index assumes a value of zero. If price exceeds marginal cost, the Lerner index becomes positive and varies between zero and unity.

Letter of Credit. A document which is issued by a bank on behalf of a customer which guarantees payment by the bank of cheques drawn by the customer, or more commonly today of bills drawn on that customer, by parties from whom he has bought goods.

Letter of Engagement. Refers to a letter which is issued by a firm of accountants to a client at the time of being engaged setting out such matters as what they understand the engagement to involve, the way in which the work will be carried out, the basis on which fees are calculated, and details of other services which the firm is able to provide.

Letter of Hypothecation. The term used for a letter from an exporter to his bank authorising it, in the event of the importer failing to accept or pay a bill of exchange, to sell the goods exported and remit the proceeds less expenses.

Letter of Representation. Refers to a letter from the directors of a company (or other entity) to an auditor placing on record the representations of management on significant matters directly affecting the accounts and financial statements.

Leverage. Means an indicator of the relationship between long-term debt and capital employed. It is measured by the ratio, long—term debt ÷ total capital employed.

Leveraged Buy-outs. Means business acquisition in which the managers of the business successfully bid and take control, in a transaction financed largely by borrowing; the debt is ultimately paid either out of the earnings of the business, or from the sale of its assets.

Leveraged Lease. In general terms, a finance lease to which there are three parties: a lessee, a lessor and a lender who provides financing to the lessor.

Lewis Model. This model describes how the transition from an agrarian to an industrialised economy has been found to depend more on a healthy, growing and cheap workforce than on conventional capital.

Liability. An obligation, which arises from a transaction or other event that has already occurred and that involves an enterprise in a probable future transfer of cash, goods or services, or the foregoing of a future cash receipt, the amount of which and the date of settlement of which are measurable with reasonable accuracy.

Lien. Means a claim against property; a bond has been usually secured by a lien against specified property of the company.

Limited Liability. It is the restriction of an owner's loss in a business to the extent of the capital that he has invested in it.

Limited Liability Company. Refers to a company the liability of whose shareholders is limited.

Limiting Factor. Synonym for Constrant.

Limit Pricing. Means the way in which established firm within an industry is able to set price with the objective of preventing new entry.

Linear Cost Function. Refers to a Cost Function which can be represented by a straight line. Accountants usually assume that cost functions are linear over a Relevant Range.

Linear Depreciation. Synonym for straightline depreciation.

Linear Expenditure Systems. In linear expenditure systems the demand functions have been expressed for groups of goods rather than for individual goods.

Liquid Assets. Refers to current assets other than stocks and work in progress (inventories). They are also referred to as Quick Assets.

Liquidation. (also known as winding-up). Refers to the process whereby the existence of a company gets terminated, its property having been realized and distributed among its creditors and in the event of a surplus, among its members.

Liquidator. A person who is appointed to conduct the winding up of a company. His functions are to realize the company's assets in the most advantageous manner, and to distribute the proceeds, first to creditors, and then, if there is any money left, to shareholders in order of priority.

Liquidity. The term used the availability of cash, and of assets readily convertible into cash (called liquid assets), to meet immediate obligations; a volume of reserves plus credit facilities, reflected in an ability to meet current financial liabilities in cash.

Liquidity Preference. Refers to the degree of preference for holding money instead of securities.

Liquidity Ratio. Refers to the ratio of the total assets of a bank which are held in the form of cash and liquid assets.

Liquidity Trap. Refers to a situation in which an increase in the money supply does not cause a fall in the interest rate but merely in an addition to idle balances; the interest elasticity of demand for money becomes infinite.

Liquid Market. Means a market where the selling and buying can be accomplished with ease, due to the presence of a large number of interested buyers and sellers.

Liquid, to Be. To hold cash.

Listed Company. A Company Limited by Shares and listed upon a recognized stock exchange.

Listed Securities. Refers to any securities of a company listed on a recognized stock exchange.

Loan. Means an advance of finance by a lender to a borrower. Interest will be normally payable on a loan, and the term to maturity (repayment) can vary from the very short to the very long.

Loanable Funds Theory of Interest. A theory which states that interest rates are determined by the supply of, and the demand for, funds available for lending. The supply of such funds has been determined mainly by:

(a) the extent of savings, and

(b) the net increase in deposit currency.

Loan Capital. A company's long-term sources of funds raised from creditors rather than shareholders.

Locational Interdependence. Means an interrelationship between firms where one firm's decision concerning a choice of location for its plant gets affected by the locational choices of its competitors.

Location Theory. Refers to that body of economic theory which analyses the forces which determine the location of economic activity, and seeks to explain and predict the spatial pattern of the location of economic agents.

Lockout. Means the closure of the workplace by the employer in an attempt to compel the employees to accede to the terms of employment which are desired by management.

Long Rate. The rate of interest, or rather set of interest rates, obtainable on long-dated securities, and therefore payable on new long-term borrowings.

Loss Contingencies. Refer to those Contingent Liabilities that are recognized in the balance sheet.

Loss on Holding Money. Refers to a loss of purchasing power that arises through holding Monetary Assets through a rise in a price level.

Loss Reliefs. Reliefs from tax granted in respect of losses. Such reliefs may be available against any income or may be restricted in some way. Tax rules may allow losses to be carried forward or back or both.

Long-run Average Cost. In the long run all cost tends to be variable costs. The long-run average cost curve will therefore relate to the minimum cost sections of a series of overlapping short-run cost curves.

Long-run Consumption Function. Refers to the functional relationship between consumption and income over periods of over 50 years. In these studies 10-year averages of income and consumption are regarded to remove the effects of the business cycle.

Long-run Marginal Cost. Means the extra cost of producting an extra unit of output in the long run.

Lorenz Curve. In measuring the income distribution of a community, a curve showing what percentage of families receive what percentage of the community's family income; the curve indicates the degree of inequality in income distribution. The Lorenz curve has other uses e.g., the measurement of concentration in industry.

Loss Leader. A good sold by a retailer below normal price, not for the purpose of making a profit on the sale of the good, but for the purpose of attracting customers likely to purchase other goods at his shop.

Luxury Taxes. Raising taxes for government funds can be very problematic in less developed countries; many people are self—employed or paid in kind and cannot be made liable for income tax.

M

Macroaccounting. By analogy with the term acroeconomics, National Accounting, i.e., those aspects of accounting concerned with nations rather than individuals or organizations.

Macro-dynamics. An area of economic study which examines the determinants of the rate of increase (or decrease) of the main categories of demand for capital or goods, consumer goods, exports, and so on.

Macro-distribution. Means distribution of national income into such broad aggregates as wages, rent, interest and profits.

Macro-economic Policy. Public policy which is concerned with the ways in which certain policy instruments such as government expenditure, the money supply, and rates of interest, may be used for achieving certain desirable targets like full employment, balance-of-payments equilibrium, and a low rate of inflation.

Macro-economics. A branch of economics which is concerned with the analysis of the economy in the large, i.e., with such large aggregates as the volume of employment, saving and investment, the national income.

Malleable Capital. The materials incorporated into a particular machine may be instantly and costlessly changed into a different machine.

Management Accounting. Refers to that part of accounting which is concerned mainly with internal reporting to the managers of an enterprise.

Management buy-out. Refers to a transaction by means of which a team of managers acquires a substantial holding in a company.

Manager-controlled Firm. A company which is having no

individual shareholder or group of shareholders owning a sufficiently high proportion of the voting stock to exert control over company policy.

Managerial Capitalism. Refers to the organization of the economy into large corporations having the power over resources located within a definable managerial class separated from the property owning class and largely independent of their control.

Managing Director. A person who is appointed as a director of a limited company.

Manpower. In economics, manpower means the organisation of work force for its utilization in different sectors of the economy.

Marginal Analysis. A tool of analysis which is found in all branches of economic theory. It in concerned with the relationships between marginal changes in related economic variables; marginal changes being very small increments or decrements in the total quantity of a variable.

Marginal Cost. Refers to the extra cost of an extra unit of production. Marginal cost is thus dependent upon Variable Costs not Fixed Costs.

Marginal Pricing. Basing prices on the marginal costs of products, i.e., (if marginal costs are constant over the relevant range), on product costs based on marginal costing (Variable Costing).

Marginal Cost Pricing. Refers to a concept in which selling prices have been brought into equality with the marginal costs of production, through variations in output.

Marginal Damage Cost. Means the extra cost of damage done, generally by pollution, from an extra unit of the nuisance-creating activity.

Marginal Disutility. Means the extra disutility which is resulting from a small change in some variable.

Marginal Efficiency of Capital. Means that unique rate of discount which would be able to make the present value of the expected net returns from a capital asset just equal to its supply price when there is no rise in the supply price of the asset.

Marginal Efficiency of Investment. It is also known as the internal rate of return. It refers to that rate of discount which would make the present value of the expected net returns from the capital asset just equal to its supply price whether it is recognized that this price will be rising in the short-run.

Marginal Firm. A firm which has been the last to enter, or the first to leave, a particular line of production.

Marginal Land. Means the land which is the last to be brought into, or the first to be taken out of, a particular line of production.

Marginal Product. Refers to the amount added to the total product by the addition of one more unit of capital-and-labour.

Marginal Productivity Doctrine. A hypothesis which states that an employer who seeks to maximize his profits will get guided by the law of diminishing marginal productivity while successive units of labour hired yield successively diminishing returns to output.

Marginal Propensity to Consume. Means the change in consumption because of an additional unit of income.

Marginal Propensity to Import. Refers to the change in imports because of a unit change in income.

Marginal Propensity to Save. Refers to the change in savings because of an additional unit of income.

Marginal Propensity to Tax. Refers to the change in tax revenues because of a unit change in income.

Marginal Propensity to Withdraw. Refers to the change in withdrawals (W) because of one additional unit of income (Y) which may be written as follows :

$$MPW = \frac{\Delta w}{\Delta Y}$$

Marginal Rate of Substitution. In consumer demand theory it refers to the amount of one good, say Y, which is needed to compensate the consumer for giving up an amount of another good, say X, such that the consumer possesses the same level of welfare (utility) as before.

Marginal Rate of Tax. Refers to the rate of tax applicable to a small increase in a taxpayer's income.

Marginal Utility. Refers to the increase or decrease in the total utility of consumption of a good which is resulted from increasing or decreasing the quantity of the good consumed by one unit.

Marginal Utility, Law of Diminishing. A proposition which states that the marginal utility of a commodity to anyone, other things being equal, diminishes after some point with every increase in his supply of it.

Marginal Utility of Money. Refers to the rate at which an individual's utility gets increased as his personal budget (income) gets expanded by one unit.

Margin of Safety. Refers to the excess of budgeted or actual sales over the breakeven sales volume.

Market. Refer to an area, however large or small, where buyers and sellers come in sufficiently close contact with each other to ensure that the price of a commodity tends to be the same in all parts of the market, allowance being made for transportation costs, tariff barriers, and other obstacles.

Marketable Securities. US term for Investments held as Current Assets.

Market Capitalization. Refers to the total value of all a listed company's shares on the stock market.

Market Clearing. Refers to situation in which the forces of supply and demand have been so in balance that all the goods have been sold i.e., the market has cleared.

Market Demand Curve. Means the aggregation of a set of individual demand curves for a good.

Market Economy. Means as economy in which the crucial economic decisions and choices have been made in a decentralised manner by numerous private individuals and firms, operating through a free price-and-market mechanism.

Market Failure. Refers to the failure of the market system to provide the optimal level of production of a good or service.

Market Forces. Refer to pressures which are produced by the free play of market supply and demand and induce adjustment in prices and or quantities traded.

Market if Touched Order. A market order executed when a transaction takes place at, or better than, a specified price after the order has been transmitted.

Marketing. A term used to cover those activities of firms which are associated with the sales and distribution of products.

Market Orientation. Refers to a tendency for producers to locate their factories near the markets in which the products will be sold rather than (say) near a raw material source.

Market Performance. Refers to the performance of a firm or industry in a market measured against specified criteria.

Market Portfolio. Refers to a Portfolio of all securities available in the securities market, weighted by their respective total market values.

Market Power. Refers to the ability of a single, or group of buyer(s) of seller(s) to influence the price of the product or service in which it is trading.

Market Price. In a stock exchange context, the price at which a listed company's securities can be bought and sold.

Market Risk. Synonym for Systematic Risk.

Market Share. Refers to the proportion of total market sales accounted for by one firm.

Market Structure. Refers to the economically significant features of a market which affect the behaviour of firms in the industry supplying that market.

Marshallian Demand Curve. The term refers to the most widely used demand curve in which the responsiveness of quantity demanded to price incorporates both the income effect and the substitution effect.

Marshallism Economics. The neo-classical economics which is associated with Alfred Marshall (1842-1924) and his follows. The more striking contributions to economic science made in his Principles of Economics were:

(a) The clarification of the respective roles played by demand and by costs of production in the determination of value;

(b) The general theory of economic equilibrium in which all the elements of the economic world are kept in their places by mutual counterpoise and interaction, a theory strengthened by two subsidiary concepts—the 'margin' and 'substitution';

(c) The explicit introduction of the element of time as a factor in economic analysis, with the concepts of the 'short' and 'long' period;

(d) The distinction between, 'external' and 'internal' economics;

(e) The doctrine of 'normal profit' assisted by the concepts of 'quasi-rent' and the representative firm'.

(f) The concept of consumer's surplus;

(g) The introduction of the idea of elasticity;

(h) Proof that laissez-faire, regarded as a principle of maximum social advantage, breaks down in certain conditions, theoretically and not merely practically; and

(i) An examination of the effects of monopoly. Marshall's successor was A.C. Pigou (1877-1959).

Marshall Lerner Condition. A devaluation of the currency may under certain conditions improve the balance of payments.

Marshall Lerner Criterion. In its simplest form, it refers to a rule which states that the price elasticities of demand for imports and exports must sum to greater than unity for an improvement to be effected in the balance of trade through a change in a country's exchange rate.

Marxist Economics. Means a school of economic thought which seeks to analyse the social and economic development of the capitalist economic system.

Marxist Socialism. A creed developed by Karl Marx (1818-1883) which had its origin in the conditions created by the Industrial Revolution.

Master Budget. Refers to a Budget which summarizes the objectives of all the sub-units of an organization.

Matching. Refers to the allocation of the financial effect of Transactions and other Events into appropriate accounting periods so that relevant income and expenditure is matched.

Materiality. Refers to the threshold for recognition of an accounting item in a financial statement.

Materials Variances. Refer to deviations from budgeted or standard cost in respect of direct materials.

Maturity. Means the date on which a loan or bond or debenture becomes due and is to be paid off, i.e., the capital refunded.

Maximum Basis. Method of calculating Earnings Per Share (EPS) which assumes that a company has distributed all its earnings and is liable to pay Advance Corporation Tax (Act) on them.

Mean Variance Rule. A decision rule which is used for evaluating capital investments on the basis of their expected returns and standard deviations (used as a measure of risk).

Memorandum of Association. Refers to a document required to be field with the Registrar of Companies when a company is incorporated.

Mercantilism. Refers to the economic philosophy of merchants and statesmen during the sixteenth and seventeenth centuries. It relied upon a strong state and the extensive regulation of economic activity.

Merchant Bank. Banks which act as Accepting Houses, Issuing Houses, company financial advisers, managers of Takeove Bids, unit trust managers, etc.

Merchanting. A type of trade which involves the buying of goods in one overseas country and selling them in another.

Merger. In general, a situation in which two or more enterprises cease to be distinct enterprises.

Merger Accounting. Refers to the preparation of Consolidated Financial Statements on the assumption that one company has merged with another rather than acquired another.

Microaccounting. By analogy with the term microeconomics, those aspects of accounting concerned with individuals and organizations rather than nations.

Micro-dynamics. An area of economic study which examines the forces governing the rates of increase (or of decrease) of demand for particular commodities, or those governing the rates of increase or decrease in the prospects of particular firms or industries.

Micro-economics. Or economics 'in the small'; a branch of economics which deals with the analysis of the behaviour of individual consumers and producers, particularly with the optimising behaviour of individual units such as households and firms.

Minority Interest. Refers to that part of the net profit or loss, or of the net assets, of a subsidiary attributable to shares owned other than by the parent company or other group company.

Mint. Refers to the place where money in coin form is made.

Mint Par of Exchange. Under a Gold Standard the relative value of the coins of different countries. The rate of exchange between two countries on the Gold Standard will only vary from this by the cost of the transport of gold between the two centres.

Mixed Good. Goods, the benefit of consuming which has been neither confined solely to one individual nor available equally to everyone.

Mixed Market Economy. Refers to a system which combines competitive private enterprise with some degree of central control.

Mordern Equivalent Asset. In Current Cost Accounting (CCA) systems, the asset which would be bought now if one were not already held.

Monetarism. Refers to a school of economic thought which argues that disturbances within the monetary sector are the principal cause of instability in the economy.

Monetary Assets. Refer to those Assets which have a fixed monetary exchange value which is not affected by a change in the price level although it may be affected by Indexation.

Monetary Policy. Refers to that part of economicy policy that regulates the level of money or liquidity in an economy with a view to achieve some desired policy objective, such as the control of inflation, improvement in the balance of payments, a certain level of employment or growth in the Gross National Product.

Monetary Theory. This terms is used to refer to the branch of macroeconomics which studies money in all its aspects.

Monetary Unit Sampling (MUS). In an audit context, a sampling plan in which the monetary unit is the sample item and is then subjected to Random Sampling or Systematic Random Sampling.

Money. The term used for anything which is widely accepted in exchange for goods, or in settling debts, not for itself but because it can be similarly passed on, has the character of money because it servey the primary function of money, i.e., a means of payment.

Money Capital. Refers to the value of the net assets of an enterprise in nominal monetary units, as in Historical Cost Accounting.

Money Market. The financial institutions which deal in short-term securities, loans, gold, and foreign exchange.

This mainly refers to the backing system.

Capital Market: Market for long-term loans. This is the opposite of money market.

Money Supply. A supply of purchasing power comprising several streams.

Money Transmission. All the ways by which the ownership of money may by transferred from one person to another in the course of making payments.

Monopolistic Competition. Refers to a market situation in which competition exists between each of two or more (perhaps numerous) sellers whose products are close, but not perfect, substitutes for one another.

Monopoly. A market structure having a single seller of a commodity or service dealing with a large number of buyers; the seller has complete control over the quantities of goods offered for sale and the price at which the goods are sold.

Monopoly Power. It is the ability of a firm or group of firms to influence the market price of the commodity or service it sells.

Monte Carlo Methods. Refers to a technique for discovering the small sample properties of econometric estimators. A hypothetical economic model with known parameters has been used to generate artificial data having known characteristics, and the estimator has been used to estimate the parameter of the model.

Moratorium. A procedure whereby major creditors individually agree not to press for payment of debts owing, on the grounds that their interests will be better served by continued trading.

Mortgage. Refers to the conveyance of property by a debtor (mortgagor to a creditor mortgagee) as security for a debt, with a condition that the property will have to be reconveyed on payment of the debt.

Mortgage Loans. Refer to loans for which specific assets in land and buildings are used as security.

Most Favoured Nation Clause. Refers to a clause in an international trade agreement which states that contracting parties to the agreement are bound to grant to each other treatment as favourable as they extend to any other country regarding the application of import and export duties and other trade regulations.

Multicollinearity. Refers to an econometric problem in which two or more of the explanatory variables in a regression analysis have been highly correlated with each other.

Multi-column Reporting. Refers to the side-by-side presentation of financial data drawn up on several different measurement bases with.

Multilateral Trade. Refers to trade among several countries, whose exports and imports have been not in balance between pairs of countries, though countries will tend to be in balance with regard to their total foreign payments and total foreign receipts.

Multinational Corporation. Means a corporation or company which is operating in a number of countries with production or service facilities outside the country of its origin; the principal decisions of the Company are taken in a global context.

Multiproduct Firm. Refers to an enterprise which combines factors of production to produce a range of products.

Mutually Exclusive Projects. Capital investment projects of which for technical reasons only one can be selected, e.g., projects to build houses or factories on the same block of land.

MV = PT. The equation of exchange of the quantity theory of money.

N

Navice Investor. Refers to on investor who lacks a good knowledge and understanding of the accounting practices and theories relevant to published financial statements and does not have ready access to a person who has such knowledge and understanding.

National Accounting. Recording the transactions, both current and capital, of a national economy, as distinct from those of entities in sectors of the economy such as public authorities and business enterprises.

National Balance Sheet. A statement which records the assets and financial obligations of an economy and its sectors at a point of time.

National Bargaining. Refers to the collective bargaining between employees and employers representatives to establish pay and conditions of work in a single industry or industry group throughout the country.

National Capital. Comprises of fixed and circulating capital used in the process of production plus the consumer's durables and other goods lying for the use of consumers or households.

National Debt. Refers to the total of outstanding debt obligations of central government and, among other distinctions. It is divided into marketable debt, i.e., securities traded on markets like the stock exchange or the discount market; and non—marketable debt, e.g., national savings certificates.

National Income. Refers to a measure of the money value of the goods and services becoming available to the nation from economic activity.

National Income and Expenditure Accounts. Accounts that show how the goods and services of a national economy are produced, distributed and either consumed or added to wealth during an accounting period.

Nationalisation. State ownership and control of any of the means of production, distribution or exchange.

Nationalized Industry. Refers to a industry which produces output for sale to consumers and other producers by way of markets but which has been solely owned by and under the control of the government.

National Wealth. Comprises of national capital and land with all the productive resources given by nature and existing in their natural state. In short, wealth includes all reproducible and irreproducible resources.

National Wealth Statement. A statement which is recording the fixed assets, stocks (inventories) and net foreign claims (positive or negative) of a national economy.

Natural Economy. Natural economy of a country comprises of its natural resources like land, climate, forests, mountains, rivers, mines etc.

Natural Monopoly. Refers to that monopoly which a country or a part of it has specially as a gift of nature. For example, gold mines at Kolar fields in Karnataka, tea gardens in Assam, etc.

Natural Rate of Growth. Refers to the rate of growth of the effective labour force in the Harrod-Domar growth model. With a fixen coefficients production function the natural rate has been the maximum sustainable rate of growth of real income. The natural rate (G_N) has been composed of the rate of growth of population (n) plus labour-augmenting technical progress (λ) (also known as Harrod-neutral technical progress). Thus

$$G_N = n + \lambda$$

Natural Resources. Refers to all the freely given material phenomena of nature within the boundaries of men's activities, at present these boundaries extend to approximately 4 miles below the earth's surface and 12 miles above it. There may be additional qualities of situation and location which can be regarded as natural resources.

Near Money. Assets which are readily convertible into money e.g., deposit accounts, deposits with savings banks and building societies, and certain short-term government securities.

Negative Gearing. Refers to a situation which arises when, for example, the interest payments due on the borrowing for an investment exceed the net revenue from the investment.

Negative Goodwill. A credit balance on Goodwill account representing an excess of the sum of the values of the enterprise's net assets taken individually over the value of the business as a whole.

Negative Income Tax. A scheme under which, if taxable income exceeds a certain amount, tax is payable whereas if it falls short of that amount a cash sum is received by the 'taxpayer' as a supplement.

Negative Real Interest Rate. Refers to an interest rate which is less than the rate of inflation.

Negotiable Instruments. Documents, such as Bills of Exchange, with the characteristics that the property in them passes by delivery, the holder in due course is not prejudiced by any defects of title on the part of the transferor or any previous holder, and the holder can sue upon them in his own name.

Negotiated Static Budget. Refers to a Static Budget arrived at after negotiation. Such budgets are normal for discretionary costs.

Neo-classical Economics. Refers to a body of economic theory which uses the general approach methods and techniques of the original nineteenth century marginalist economics.

Neo-classical Equilibrium. A concept of neo-classical economics in which the equilibrium between production and purchasing power got established at a level where all willing and useful workers had been employed.

Neo-classical Growth Theory. A general term which refers to the models of economic growth developed in a neo-classical frame-work, where the emphasis has been placed on the case of substitution between capital and labour in the production function to ensure steady-state growth, so that the problem of instability found in the Harrod—Domar Growth Model because of the assumed fixed capital to labour coefficients is avoided.

Neo-classical Model. Refers to a view of the economy held in whole or substantial part by the neo-classical economists; the essentials of the system appeared to be as follows.

Netback. Synonym for Recoverable Amount.

Net Basis. Method of calculating Earnings Per Share (EPS) which takes account of all the components, both constant and variable, in a company's tax charge.

Net Current Assets. Current Assets less Current Liabilities.

Net Book Value. A statement of the value of fixed assets which is used in accounting.

Net Demostic Product (NDP). Gross Domestic Product minus depreciation.

Net Investment. Means the addition to the economy's total capital stock, i.e. the amount of investment net of depreciation. It is also known as net capital formation.

Net National Product. Gross National Product less Capital Consumption (depreciation).

Net Present Value (NPV). The discounted value of the future incremental cash receipts expected from the use of an asset less the discounted value of the incremental cash outlays.

Net Profit. Refers to the excess of revenues over expenses. It may be calculated before or after extraordinary items and before or after tax depending upon the context.

Net Profit Ratio. Refers to the ratio of net profit to sales.

Net Realizable Value. Refers to the amount of money for which an asset can be exchanged in a market, i.e., selling price less selling costs.

Neutrality. In an accounting context, the absence in reported information of bias intended to attain a predetermined result or to induce a particular mode of behaviour.

Neutrality of Money. It is a theorem which states that via the operation of the real balance effect in the money market, there will exist an equal proportionate increase in equilibrium money prices for a given increase in the money supply.

New Combridge School. The term used for a school of economists which have been associated with certain members of the Cambridge Economic Policy Group at the Department of Applied Economics. university of Cambridge Since the 1970s the school has made a number of distinct analytical contributions concerned with the long-run behaviour of the economy.

New Classical School. A school of economies which has been associated with the names of Lucas, Sargent and Minford. The School believes that (1) expectations are rational, and (2) markets clear very quickly when wages and prices are flexible, up and down.

'New Classical Macroeconomics'. It is a restatement in a more rigorous form of orthodox classical economics. This restatement is based on the notion of rational expectation combined with a natural rate of unemployment which emerges because of efficient market clearing.

New Economic Policy. A term which was used to describe the workings of the economic system in the USSR in the 1920s.

'New Economics'. Descriptive of the analytical and philiosophical approach to economic policy-making used by the Kennedy and Johnson adminstrations in the 1960s.

New Keynesian School. A school of economics which is associated with the names of Klein, Tobin, Hicks, and Meade. In common with monetarists, its adherents believed that economies tend towards a full employment equilibrium.

'New Microeconomics'. The name assigned to a body of economic literature which has sought to identify the microeconomics of macroeconomics; specifically, to offer a firm microeconomic rationale of the mechanisms underlying the aggregate relationships between price changes and unemployment.

Normal Good. A good whose demand gets reduced as income falls.

Normal Price. Means the long-run price of a commodity. It is defined by Alfred Marshall as the 'value which economic forces would bring about if the general conditions of life were stationary for a run of time long enough to enable them all to work out their full effect'.

Normal Profits. Refer to that minimum amount of profit which a firm must acquire so as to induce the firm to remain in operation.

Normative Economics. Economic studies consisting of statements on what individual business or public policy ought to be, the statements being based upon the value-judgments of the economist concerned.

Notes to the Accounts. Information relating to the financial statements not given on the face of the statements.

O

OAPEC. Abbreviation of Organization of Arab Petroleum Exporting Countries.

Objectivity. Refers to an accounting concept which stresses the need to establish rules for recording financial transactions which as far as possible do not depend upon the personal judgment of the measurer.

Obsolescence. Refers to the decline in value of a fixed asset through external causes such as technological change or changes in demand.

Occupational Mobility. The mobility which is prevalent in an economy and provides for inter-change of work force from one occupation to another.

Off Balance Sheet Financing. Financing assets by 'borrowing' in such a fashion that the debt does not appear as a balance sheet item.

Offer. Means the price at which a person is ready to sell as opposed to bid, the price at which one is ready to buy.

Offer for Sale. Refers to an offer to the public, either by an issuing house or by a stockbroker, of securities already in issue or for which the issuing house or the broker has agreed to subscribe.

Offsetting Contract. A futures contract which offsets or closes out an earlier obligation to deliver or take delivery of the commodity in question.

Ohlin's Theory of Relative Price Difference. According to this theory, relative price differences result in the absolute price difference where a rate of exchange has been settled. These differences indicate in what commodities each region should specialize. The rate of exchange and the value of interregional and international trade has been determined by reciprocal demand. Ohlin extended his analysis to any number of regions or nations without in any way alternating its basic methods or conclusions.

Oil and Gas Accounting. Accounting for the acquisition, exploration, development and production phases of the exploitation of oil and gas deposits and for proved oil and gas reserves.

Oligopolistic Behaviour. Means conduct by firms which is characterized by perceived interdependence in decision marking with regard to major policy areas like pricing, advertising and investment.

Oligopoly. The term refers to a market structure within which firms have been aware of the mutual interdependance of sales, production, investment and advertising plans.

Oligopsony. Means a market in which a few buyers have to face a very large number of sellers. This type of market is comparable to that of oligopoly.

One Sector Growth Model. A model which is used in growth theory where a single homogeneous product is produced which is equally useful as a consumption of as an investment goods.

OPEC. Abbreviation of Organization of Petroleum Exporting Countries.

Open Contracts. In a commodity market contracts which have been bought or sold without the transaction having been completed by subsequent sale or purchase, or by making or taking actual delivery of the financial instrument of physical commodity.

Open Economy. An economy which has been engaging in international trade. The degree of openness of an economy may be approximated by the size of its foreign trade sector relative to its gross domestic product.

Open Interest. The total number of futures contracts, whether purchased or sold, recorded on the books of a commodity exchange which are not offset by the opposite transactions or by physical delivery of the commodity.

Open Market. Open market in the context of world economy implies that a country permits international exchange of goods and services and currencies without much restriction.

Open Market Value. Refers to the value on the open market of non—specialized buildings and land.

Operating Budget. Refers to that part of the Master Budget of an organization that deals with operations.

Operating Cost Ratio. Operating costs which are expressed as a proportion of the value of net sales.

Operating Income. The income which arises out of the normal business of a firm.

Operating Leverage. Refers to the Gearing (Leverage) which results from an enterprise's asset structure as distinct from its Capital Structure.

Operating Profit. Refers to that profit which would be earned if no resources get diverted to the future expansion of the firm.

Operating Ratios. Ratios which indicate the operating efficiency of a business. Examples of operating ratios are:

$$\frac{\text{Cost of Sales}}{\text{Stock (including stores and work in progress)}}$$

$$\frac{\text{Stock of Furnished Goods}}{\text{Production costs for period}}$$

$$\frac{\text{Trade Creditors}}{\text{purchasers}}$$

Operational Audit. Refers to that branch of Internal Audit concerned with non-financial as well as financial performance and with evaluating efficiency and effectiveness.

Operation Costing. Refers to a hybrid of Process Costing and Job Costing, used in the manufacture of goods that are produced in batches.

Opportunity Cost. Refers to the maximum contribution that is foregone by using scarce resources for a particular purpose.

Opportunity Value. Synonym for Value to the Business.

Optimisation. A key concept in micro-economics; the consumer is assumed to maximum utility or satisfaction, subject to the constraints of income, while the producer is assumed to maximise profit and minimise costs, subject to the technological and legal constraints within which it operates.

Optimum Firm. Means a firm in which the costs of production per unit of output have been at a minimum having regard to the existing state of technical knowledge and managerial ability.

Optimum Plant Size. Refers to that size of plant at which long-run average costs have been at a minimum.

Optimum Tariff. Refers to the name given to the tariff which maximizes the welfare or utility enjoyed by a nation.

Option. A contract which is giving the right to buy or sell securities or commodities within or at the end of a given time period at an agreed price.

Ordinary Shares. Refers to those shares on the holders of which are normally conferred the residue of rights which have not been conferred on other classes of shares.

Organisation. Organisation means the place where some economic process/activity-trade or industry has been carried on.

Outlay Cost. A cost arising from a disbursement of cash.

Output. Refers to the end product of transforming inputs into goods.

Output Budgeting. Means a system of accounting which classifies costs according to the outputs in the production of which they are incurred rather than in terms of the inputs which are purchased.

Outside Money. The money which is backed by assets which are not debts in that the assets do not represent a claim on individuals within the economy.

Outstanding Capital Stock. Refers to the capital stock of a corporation in the hands of the public.

Outturn. The actual expenditure incurred, normally in a financial year.

Overabsorbed Overhead. A credit balance resulting from the use of Predetermined Overhead Rates.

Overdraft. Refers to a system of bank lending, by which the borrower is permitted to draw cheques beyond the credit balance in his account, up to an agreed limit, and to pay interest only on the daily amounts by which his account is overdrawn.

Overheads. Costs which are not directly chargeable to any unit produced.

Overhead Variances. Deviations from budgeted or standard costs in respect of overheads.

Overnight Money. Refers to money which is lent in one or other of the money markets, at the very shortest term of recall.

Overtrading. Means a situation in which a firm has little working capital.

Overvalued Currency. Means a currency whose exchange rate is fixed above the free market equilibrium rate.

Owner's Equity. That part of the finance of an enterprise provided by its owners.

Own Shares. A company's own shares acquired by purchase, redemption, gift, surrender or forfeiture.

P

Paasche Index. An index which is used for measuring changes, e.g. in prices. It uses current period weights, but since current year weights are seldom known, the index is difficult to construct. The index uses the following method.

$$\frac{\Sigma P_n q_n}{\Sigma P_o q_n}$$

where P_o= price in the base-year, P_n= price in the year under consideration; and q_n= quantity in the year under consideration. The index has the disadvantage that in times of generally rising prices it tends to underestimate price increases.

Paid-up Capital. That part of the issued capital which is paid up by the shareholders.

Paid-up Share Capital. The Issued Share Capital to the extent that it has been called up from the shareholders and cash or other consideration has been received from them.

Paper Money. General term which is used for money in the form of banknotes. Under a gold standard these are convertible into gold coin or bullion; otherwise they are inconvertible.

Paper Enterpreneur. A business organiser who is applying the skills of the enterpreneur to the task of achieving short-term profits for the firm, not through new productive investment but through strategies involving simply the rearrangement of assets and the clever manipulation of rules and numbers, shrewed manoeuvring the transfer of losses from the firm to the public through a successful plea for public subsidies or tax concessions, threats of legal actions and takeovers, and the finishing of accounts and taxation returns.

Paper Gold. See special drawing rights.

Paper Profits. Refers to profits that cannot be or have not been realized in cash or that result from using Historical Cost Accounting rather than some form of Inflation Accounting.

Parent Company. A company which controls another company.

Pareto Improvement. Refers to reallocation of resources which makes at least one person better of without making anyone worse off.

Pareto's Law. It is an empirical relationship which describes the number of persons whose income is x in a given population, advanced by Vilfredo Pareto (1848-1923). Italian economist and sociologist. Pareto concluded from his studies that national income had an inevitable tendency to be distributed in the some way regardless of social and political institutions and system of taxation.

Par Rate of Exchange. Refers to the expression of exchange rates in terms of gold or dollars.

Partial Equilibrium. Refers to the study of a market for a commodity in isolation. Given the prices of all other commodities the conditions for equilibrium in a single market could be examined. This technique was used by A. Marshall.

Partial Equilibrium Analysis. Economic analysis of a small sector of an economy such as the market for a particular commodity, in which the prices of several or all other commodities are held fixed relative to one another, and spillovers between markets are largely ignored.

Participative Budgeting. Allowing persons who will be responsible for performance under a Budget to participate in the decisions by which the budget is established.

Partnership Accounts. The accounts and financial statements of an unincorporated business or professional enterprise owned by two or more persons.

Par Value. The face value or nominal value of a share or a debenture.

Pay As You Earn (PAYE). The mechanism used for withholding tax from wages and salaries. Unlike similar systems used elsewhere it is operated on a cumulative basis, i.e., a taxpayer's pay and allowances are accumulated throughout the tax year so that the amount withheld in any one period is dependent on the income received throughout the year up to and including the current period.

Pay-back Method. It is method which is used for comparing the profitability of alternative projects, the object has been to determine over what period the net cash generated by an investment will repay the cost of the project

$$\text{Pay-back peroid} = \frac{\text{Cost of Project}}{\text{Annual Increase in income (after tax)}}$$

Payback Period. Refers to a method of Capital Investment Appraisal, which measures the expected length of time over which the undiscounted cash receipts of a capital project equal the undiscounted outlays.

Pay Ceiling. Refers to an effective upper-limit on the size of pay settlements. A pay ceiling may come to be considered as the norm or the going rate.

Payment-by-results. The term used for systems of payment under which the worker is paid according to the volume of output he or the work group or plant of which he is part produces. It is also known as incentive payment systems.

Pay-off. Refers to the net benefit that occurs when a particular course of action has been taken.

Payout Ratio. Means the percentage of the firm's net profit which is paid out as dividends.

Payroll Accounting. Accounting for wages and salaries.

Pecuniary External Economy. The term used for a situation where the profits of a firm depend not only on its own inputs and outputs but also on the inputs and outputs of other firms.

Per Capita. Per head, e.g. per capital national income—the average level of national income for each member of the population.

Per Capita Income. The average distribution of the Net National Product of a country over the total population of the country.

Perfect Competition. A market structure is considered to be perfectly competitive if the following conditions hold; there are a large number of firms each with an insubstantial share of the market. These firms produce a homogeneous product using identical production processes and have perfect information. It is also the case that there is free entry to the industry, that is new firms can and will enter the industry if they observe that greater than normal profits are being earned. The main effect of this free entry has been to push the demand curve facing each firm downwards until each firm earns only normal profits, at which point there exists no further incentive for new entrants to come into the industry. Further since each firm produces a homogeneous product, it cannot be able to raise its price without losing all of its market to its competitors. Hence the demand curve facing each firm in the long-run will be horizontal and tangential to the minimum point of the long-run average cost curve of the firm.

Perfect Market. In an accounting and financial context, a market in which there are no transactions costs, no firm or individual has any special advantage or opportunity to earn abnormal returns on investments, and prices are not affected by the actions of any individual or firm.

Performance Evaluation. The assessment by a superior of a subordinate and an important part of any Management Control system.

Performance Report. A report which is comparing actual with budgeted performance.

Period Costs. Costs that cannot be identified with goods acquired or produced for sale.

Periodic Inventory Method. A method under which the amount of inventory (stock) on hand and hence the cost of goods sold is determined by means of physical counts at periodic intervals.

Permanent Differences. Differences, not reversible in future periods, between profits as computed for taxation purposes and profits as stated in financial statements.

Permanent-income Theory of Consumption. A theory which was developed by Milton Friedman (p.1912). According to this theory people gear their consumption behaviour to their permanent or long-term consumption opportunities, and not to their current level of income. In its simplest form this hypothesis of consumption behaviour may be put as follows:

$$C = cY^p$$

where Y^p denotes permanent disposable income, land C consumption. This consumption varies in the same proportion as permanent income, a 10 per cent increase in permanent incomes raises consumption by 10 per cent.

Perpetual Inventory Method. A method of accounting for inventories (stocks) which involves the continual recording of additions to and issues or sales of materials on a daily basis.

Perpetuity. An Annuity which lasts for ever. The present value of a perpetuity is equal to the annual receipt or payment divided by the rate of interest.

Personal Accounts. Those accounts in a ledger which record transactions with persons, e.g., debtors and creditors.

Personal Income. Refers to the flow of income that accrues to the individual or household.

Personal Ledger. A Ledger containing Personal Accounts. The most common examples are the Debtors Ledger and the Creditors Ledger.

Personalty. Movable property such as cash and shares, in contradistinction to Realty or immovable property.

Personal Savings. Refers to that part of personal income which is neither paid out in taxes not spent on goods and services (a current consumption).

Pett Cash. Cash balances held in the form of notes and coins rather than bank deposits and used in payment of minor expenditures.

Petty Cash Book. A book recording Petty Cash transactions. It is usually kept by the imprest system, in which a fixed sum or 'float' is allocated as sufficient to meet petty cash expenditure for an agreed period of time.

Petty's Law. Refers to a statement of the tendency for the proportion of the working population engaged in service industry to increase with economic development.

Phillips Curve. The statistical observation by A.W. Phillips (1958) that there occurred an inverse relationship between the rate of change of money wage rates and the unemployment rate in the UK over the period 1861-1957. That is,

$$\Delta W_t = f(U)_t$$

where ΔW denotes the change in money wage rates and U the employment rate in period *t.*

Physical Quality of Living Index. The standard of living of a country assessed taking into account the level of nutrition, standard of medical care, etc. The three main indicators are life expectancy, infant mortality, and literacy.

Physiocrats. A school of economic theory which got developed in France in the eighteenth century. Associated principally with the names of F. Quesnary and Turgot. They criticized the Merantilist belief that wealth got created in exchange and gave production pride of place in its creation. They identified the surplus over the resources used up in production as the source of accumulation. The surplus, or 'produit net' had been a surplus of material wealth produced by labour in conjunction with land.

Their analysis got limited by this concentration on agriculture which they identified as the source of all wealth.

Pigon Effect or Real Balance Effect. Means a change in expenditure which is caused by a change in the value of money holding that occurs as a consequence of changes in prices.

Pigovian Tax. Refers to a tax levied on the producer of an externality in such a way that after the tax has been introduced the private costs, as perceived by the externality-generating party, have been equal to the social costs of the activity.

Pivot Effect Hypothesis. Refers to the argument that incomes policy not only creates shift effects in the wage adjustment process.

Placing. The sale of, or the obtaining of subscriptions for, securities by either an issuing house or a stockbroker through the stock market and to or by its own clients.

Plan Comptable. French term for Accounting Plan.

Planning, Programming, Budgeting System (PPBS). A system of governmental budgeting which involves the identification of goals and objectives in each major area of governmental activity.

Planned Economy. Means an economy where crucial economic processes have been determined to a large extent not by market forces.

Planometrics. A branch of economics which is specifically concerned with the construction of optimal macroeconomic plans L.V. Kantorovich is one of the pioneers in this area using sophisticated mathematical techniques to demonstrate the possibility of efficient central planning using programming prices of 'objectively determined valuations'.

Plant Bargaining. Refers to collective bargaining between a single employer from a single plant and employee's representatives to establish rates to pay and conditions of work in that plant.

Ploughed Back Profit. Profit retained for reinvestment instead of being distributed to owners.

Politicization of Accounting. The settlement of accounting questions and the determination of accounting standards by 'political' pressures (in the widest sense) rather than by reference to an implicit or explicit Conceptual Framework.

Policy Instruments. Refer to economic and social variables which are manipulated by the government to influence policy variables. Frequently reffered to solely as instruments it is possible to distinguish four main economic categories; fiscal policy, monetary policy, exchange rate policy and most recently the direct control of prices and incomes policy.

Policy-off. Refers to period of 'free collective bargaining'. Periods in which no incomes policy are able to operate.

Policy-on. Refers to periods in which an incomes policy is in operation.

Political Economy. The term has connotations of the interrelationship between the practical aspects of political action and the pure theory of economics.

Politico-Economic Models. Refer to models which facilitate the study of how the state of the economy influences the policy, and how political behaviour influences the economy.

Poll. A method of voting whereby each member of a company can vote for or against a resolution according to the number of shares that he or she owns.

Poll Tax. A tax whose size bears no relationship to any Tax Base except the existence of the taxpayer.

Polluter Pays Principle. This principle states that the polluter should pay for polluting the environment.

Pollution Rights. Mean the idea that certificates should be issued which provided the owner a 'right of pollute' in a given environment, say—river.

Portfolio. In a financial context, a collection of different securities or other assets held by an individual or an institution which can be evaluated in terms of their combined risks and returns.

Portfolio Risks. A risk that depends not only on the riskiness of the individual securities or other assets of a portfolio but also on the relationship among those securities.

Post Balance Sheet Events. Events, both favourable, and unfavourable, which occur between the date of a balance sheet and the date on which the financial statements are approved by the board of directors.

Positive Economics. Refers to that part of economic science which deals itself with statements that are capable of verification by reference to the facts.

Post Balance Sheet Events Review. Auditing procedures applied to the period between completing the basic audit fieldwork and the audit approval of the financial statements.

Post-completion Audit. An audit of a capital project after its completion, comparing budget estimates with actual results and enquiring into the reasons for any variances.

Posting. Refers to the transferring of an amount and its description from a Journal to a Ledger.

Potential Entry. For a particular industry, refers to the possibility of new competition from firms who are not currently producing competing products.

Potential Output. Refers to the maximum feasible output of a firm, industry, sector of an economy or economy as a whole, given its factor endowments.

Poverty. Poverty can be regarded as an absolute or a relative concept. The absolute poverty approach defines minimum levels of income needed to sustain life; for example, estimating minimum dietary requires and how these can be most cheaply met. The relative poverty approach defines poverty relative to appropriate comparator groups.

Pre-acquisition Profits. The retained profits as at the date of acquisition of a company acquired by another company.

Precautionary Motive. Refers to one of the motives for holding money, i.e. as a precaution against some unforeseen circumstance occurring which would otherwise necessitate transferring wealth from some non-liquid from that may incur high transaction costs or may take too long.

Predatory Pricing. Means the practice of driving prices down to unprofitable levels for a period so as to weaken or eliminate existing competitors.

Predetermined Overhead Rate. Refers to an overhead rate estimated in advance in order that jobs and processes may be charged with a share of factory overhead without having to wait for details of overhead actually incurred.

Predictive Ability. Refers to the ability of an accounting number to provide information that is useful in predicting future accounting numbers.

Pre-emption Right. The entitlement of an existing shareholder to have allotted to him or her a proportionate part of a new issue of shares.

Preference Shares. The Shares which carry preferential rights in relation to other shares but which often do not carry voting rights.

Preferred Stock. US term for Preference Shares.

Preliminary Expenses. The expenses of forming a company, such as legal costs, registration fees, stamp duty and printing charges.

Prepayments. Expenses (e.g. insurance) which have been paid for but the benefits of which have not been received at the balance sheet date.

Price Mechanism. System which is used in a competitive society for the distribution of scarce resources through the agency of price.

Price-push. The name assigned to a type of inflation, similar to cost-push where entrepreneurs have been blamed for making inflation by charging unnecessarily high prices in order to make large profits.

Price-Setter. A firm operating in a non-competitive market faces a downward-sloping demand curve for its product and is thus having some discretion to select the price at which it sells, rather than having to be a price taker.

Price Shading. Refers to the practice of selling below published prices.

Price Support Scheme. The term used for a method which is used for artificially raising the price of a good in the market. This will result in a situation in which supply exceeds demand and would therefore normally result in the government agency responsible for the support having to purchase the excess supplies itself.

Price Theory or Micro-economic Theory. This theory is concerned with how the price system handles the problem of allocating scarce resources in a market economy.

Primary Goods. As defined in the theory of justice developed by John Rawls, these goods have been the basic rights, freedoms, income and wealth which are available for distribution in a society.

Primary Market. The principal underlying market for a financial instrument or physical commodity.

Primary Money. Another name for base money or high powered money, i.e. the money which is issued by the monetary authorities.

Prime Cost. The sum of Direct Materials and Direct Labour.

Prime Credits. Large financially strong corporations of excellent credit standing and able to sell commercial paper in the money markets.

Prime Rate. The lowest interest rate which is payable by borrowers having the highest credit rating.

Principal. Means the sum of money which is paid to the holder of a bond upon maturity to extinguish the liability.

Prior Charges. Claims on a company's assets and profits that rank ahead of those of the ordinary shareholders.

Priority Budget. An Incremental Budget in which budget requests must be accompanied by a statement of what changes would occur if last year's budget amount were increased or decreased by a certain percentage.

Priority Percentage. A method of calculating Gearing (Leverage) by computing the percentage of earnings that is required to service each category of loan and share capital.

Private Company. A company which is not a Public Company. A private company is not permitted to issue shares or debentures to the public.

Private Ledger. A ledger containing confidential accounts.

Private Sector. The 'private sector' of the economy has been the combination of elements in the economy which have been not organs or agencies of central or local government and therefore includes the company sector and the personal sector.

Privatisation. Refers to the selling back to the private sector of government assets, like nationalised industries, share stakes owned in private companies, testing stations, research centres, publicity-owned shopping centres and bus services.

Probability Proportional to Size (PPS) Sampling. In an audit context, a method of drawing a sample in which the probability of each sample unit being selected is not random but proportional to its size.

Process Costing. Refers to a costing system which is used by organizations whose products or services are mass produced in continuous fashion through a series of processes, each of which receives varying inputs of direct materials, direct labour and factory overhead, which are charged to each process rather than to individual jobs or batches. Contrast Job Costing and Operation Costing.

Procurement price. Is the price at which the government agencies compulsorily purchase a commodity according to fixed quota from the producers.

Market price is generally below the support price and above the procurement price.

Producer Sovereignty. Refers to the dominance of large producers within the economy and their ability to manage the demand for major public goods.

Producer's Surplus. Refers to the excess of the total earnings of a supplier of a good or service over the payment actually necessary to just induce him to continue to supply the amount involved. It has been the excess of revenue over the total avoidable costs of supply. The term was given by Alfred Marshall (1841-1924).

Product Costs. Costs identified with goods acquired or produced for sale. In relation to a manufactured product, product costs comprise Direct Materials, Direct Labour and Factory Overhead.

Product Cycle. The term used for the pattern of experience of new products, thus subsequently pass through the phases of matuing product and standardized product. New goods have to be developed for high income, high labour-cost countries, which briefly possess a monopoly in their production and export.

Production, Theory of. A branch of economics which is concerned with the study of alternative production methods and the consequences of decisions taken in respect of production methods.

Productivity. Means output per unit of input employed. Increases in productivity come about from increased efficiency on the part of capital or labour.

Product Market. Means the market in which goods and services have been bought and sold in a private economy.

Professional Ethics. The rules of conduct of a Profession. Accountancy Bodies may impose such rules on their members or may issue guidelines.

Profit. A general term for the excess of revenues over expenses.

Profitability Index. A variant of the Net Present Value method of Capital Investment Appraisal. The index is derived by dividing the present value of the expected cash receipts by the expected cash payments at the commencement of the project.

Profit and Loss Account Formats. Methods of presenting the items in a Profit And Loss Account.

Profit And Loss Account/Statement. A financial statement of an enterprise's revenues, expenses and profit. The format of the profit and loss accounts of companies is regulated by law and includes a profit appropriation section.

Profit and Loss Appropriation Account/Statement. Refers to an account or statement prepared by partnership and companies that discloses how the net profit or loss for the year (augmented in the case of companies but not partnerships by previously accumulated profits or losses) has been or is intended to be dealt with.

Profit Centre. A segment of a business which is held responsible for both revenues and costs.

Profit Margin. Refers to profit per unit of output which is expressed as a percentage of price.

Profit Maximization. The term used for the hypothesis that firms aim to maximize profits.

Profit Rate. Profit which is expressed as a proportion of the book value of capital assests.

Profits. Refers to the difference between 'the revenue generated from the sale of output and the full opportunity costs of the factors used in the production of that output.

Profits Push Inflation. Refers to a variant cost-push inflation, which attributes the origins of the inflationary process to capitalists who seek an enhanced share of the national income.

Pro Forma Financial Statements. Financial statements prepared for future periods on the basis of assumptions contained in Budgets.

Programme Evaluation and Review Technique (PERT). A form of Network Analysis suited to projects where there are uncertainties.

Progressive Tax. Refers to a tax that takes an increasing proportion of a taxpayer's income (or other tax base) as his or her income rises.

Project Financing. A form of lending increasingly used for natural resource developments, where more emphasis has been placed on the borrower's future cash flow for repayments, rather than an immediate assets.

Proletariat. Refers to a class of persons which owns little or no property. The distinguishing characteristic of such a group has been the necessity for them to sell their labour services in return for wages.

Promissory Note. Means a promise to pay a certain sum at a stated time, in documentary form. Depending upon its credit standing such a note has been negotiable.

Propensities to Consume and Save. Concepts which were developed by John Maynard Keynes (1883-1946). These represent the fractions of the total proceeds or income derived from employment which are, respectively, consumed and invested.

Property Rights. The rights, which pertain to the permissible use of resources, goods and services. Ownership of an assets is having the following rights: to use that asset, to change its form and substance and to transfer all rights through sale.

Proportional Tax. A tax that takes a constant proportion of a taxpayer's income (or other tax base) as his income rises.

Propulsive Industries. A group of key industries whose interaction and expansion can offer a stimulus to growth in an economy.

Prospectus. Refers to any prospectus, notice, circular, advertisement or other invitation, offering to the public for subscription or purchase any share or debentures of a company.

Provision for Depreciation. Refers to any amount written off a fixed asset and accumulated over the life of the asset.

Provisions. Either Provisions for Liabilities and Charges or valuation adjustments, i.e., amounts written off fixed assets (by way of depreciation or amortization) or current assets (e.g., a provision for Doubtful Debts).

Provisions for Liabilities and Charges. The amounts retained as reasonably necessary for the purpose of providing for any liability or loss which is either likely to be incurred, or certain to be incurred, but uncertain as to amount or as to the date on which it will arise.

Proxy. A person who is authorized to attend and vote at a company meeting on behalf of a share holder or stockholder, or the form signed by the latter, which grants that authority.

Proxy Variable. Refers to the taking of unemployment or some other variable as a 'proxy' for demand, instead of directly measuring demand forces.

Public Choice. A branch of economics which deals with the application of economics to the analysis of 'non-market' decision making. It may also be considered as an economic analysis of politics.

Public Company. See Company.

Public Debt Ratio. Refers to the ratio of public money debt in a nation which is expressed as a ratio of gross national product (G.N.P.).

Public Expenditure. Broadly, expenditures which are made by local and national government agencies as distinct from those of private individuals, organizations or firms.

Public Finance. Refers to the traditional name for the revenue and expenditure activities of government.

Public Good. A good with the characteristics that (a) individuals cannot be excluded from consuming it, even if they do not pay for it; (b) consumption by one individual does not prevent anyone else from consuming it.

Purchases Journal. Refers to a book or other record containing a chronological list of credit purchases. Each entry in the journal is credited to an account in the Creditors Ledger.

Purchases Ledger. Synonym for Creditors Ledger.

Purchasing Power Loss or Gain. A Holding Gain or loss arising from holding net Monetary Assets through a period of change in the general price level.

Purchasing Power Parity. Means a theory having little practical validity which considers the equilibrium exchange rate between two currencies to be when they have equivalent domestic purchasing power.

Purchasing Power Parity (PPP) Theorem. The theorem that, between two countries, changes in the exchange rate are proportional to changes in the relative price levels.

Purchase Tax. A type of sales tax.

Pure Competition. Refers to a large number of small firms selling a homogeneous product.

Pure Monopoly. Refers to a situation in which a single seller offers a product which has no close substitutes.

Put Option. The Buyer (taker) acquires the right to sell a futures contract at a basis (or strike) price agreed at the time of concluding the contract.

Pure Profit. Refers to a residual sum left over when we have subtracted from the revenue generated by some activity all of the opportunity costs of production, the normal profit needed to keep the producer in business.

Pushfulness. Refers to the propensity of union to engage in a wage push, i.e., their mood for militant action.

Put, To. To Sell.

Puts. A holder's option to sell.

P/V Chart. A chart which measures profit on the vertical axis and volume in physical or monetary units on the horizontal.

Pyramid Selling. Refers to a selling technique which involves a company selling the right to sell a product, or the right to sell the right to sell a product.

Q

Q-ratio. This term divised by professor James Tobin (1981 Nobel Memorial prize in economics). It is a ratio, derived empirically which measures the relationship of the market value of physical capital (such as existing plant or other corporate asset) to its replacement cost. If the Q-ratio is low corporations tend to acquire existing assets rather than build new plant and equipment. High interest rates may make existing assets look cheap and expense to replace.

Qualitative Characteristics of Accounting Information. Those characteristics that accounting information should have in order to be of maximum usefulness to readers of accounting reports.

Quality Control. Policies and procedures used to determine and maintain a desired quality of goods and services.

Quantity Theory of Money. A theory which was developed by the American economist Irving Fisher (1867-1947) the essentials of which have been contained in the equation.

$$MV = PT$$

where M = the amount of money (bank notes, etc. plus bank deposits), V = the velocity of circulation, P = a price index covering all transactions, and T = total volume of transactions per unit of time.

The equation is useful in indicating the relationship between the four parameters. This suggests that inflation could be controlled by the monetary authorities through the regulation of the quantity of money in existence. If a certain growth in real income is anticipated, this can be realised without inflation by allowing the quantity of money in the economy to increase at the same rate.

Quasi-rent. Means the return to a seller of a good or service over and above its opportunity cost when the good is temporarily in fixed supply. The concept was applied by Alfred Marshall to the determination of the price of capital in the short run when the supply of capital has been fixed.

Questionable Payments. Bribes and other payments made to foreign governments or persons in order to obtain contracts.

Queueing, Theory of. Theory dealing with the rates at which productive facilities and services should be provided so as to achieve optimum efficiency, e.g. to minimise queues' or bottlenecks and synchronise better the supply of facilities or services with the demand for them.

Quick Assets. Current assets less stocks (inventories) i.e. mainly bank balances, debtors and readily realizable investments. They are also referred to as liquid assets.

Quick Assets Ratio. Refers to the ratio of liquid asstes to current liabilities. Liquid assets include cash, most term investments which can be quickly realized and accounts receivable where an allowance is made for bad debts.

Quick Ratio. Refers to the relationship between quick assets and current liabilities. Also known as the acid test, or liquid ratio, it is widely regarded as the most useful single test of liquidity.

Quota. Means an imposed limit on the quantity of goods which are produced or purchased.

Quoted Companies. The term used for those companies whose share capital can be freely dealt in on the stock exchange.

R

Radical Economics. The generic name which is used for writing in a socialist or Marxist tradition, relating in the main to Marxism but adopting and using other sources of ideas such as anarchism and libertarianism.

Raider Firm. The term used for a company which is having the potential to establish itself as a takeover threat to another company.

Rally. A brisk rise which follows a decline in the general price level of a security market, or of an individual stock or share.

Random Sampling. In an audit context, a method of drawing a sample in which each item in the population, e.g., the purchase invoices for May, has an equal chance of being selected.

Random Walk Hypothesis. The hypothesis that share prices move independently of previous movements.

Range. Means the difference between the highest and the lowest price at which a given futures contract has traded during a particular period of time.

Range (of a Good). In regional or spatial economics, it refers to the maximum distance which people will travel for the purpose of buying a particular good.

Ratchet Theory of Pricing. This theory is a view that manufacturers tend to raise prices when costs rise, but do not reduce them when costs fall.

Rate of Interest. The term used for the price of money services. While financial markets exhibit a range of rates of interest the theory of the rate of interest explains the determinants of the 'pure' rate of interest which has been the price that would have to be paid to borrow money so as to undertake a complete riskless enterprise.

Rate of Return. A general concept which refers to the earnings from the investment of capital, where the earnings have expressed as a proportion of the outlay.

Rateable Value. A value placed on all properties subject to Rates.

Rate of Return Pricing. Basing prices on a planned rate of return on capital employed.

Rate of Surplus Value. In the Marxian scheme it refers to the ratio which surplus value bears to variable capital. Marx considered this as an expression for the degree of exploitation of labour by capital.

Rates. A local property tax levied by certain local authorities.

Rate Support Grant. The term used for a mechanism for transferring funds from the national government to local authorities.

Rational Expectations School. This term used for a group of economists who, disenchanted with the failures of microeconomic policies in the 1970s. The rational expectations school believes that there need be no involuntary unemployment, for anyone can fine work by asking for it at a wage below the existing wage.

Rationing. The term used for any method of allocating a scarce product or service other than by means of the price mechanism.

R, D and D. Research, Development and Demonstration.

Reaction Functions. Specifies for any one firm the optimum value for a choice variable given the value chosen by competitors.

Real Accounts. Refers to those accounts in a ledger which record transactions involving Non Monetary Assets, e.g., plant and machinery.

Realization Account. An account which is used on the dissolution of a partnership. The book value of assets to be sold is transferred to the debit of realization account and the proceeds of sale are placed to its credit.

Real Balance Effect. Generally the term used to describe the situation where there exists a change in the demand for commodities because of a change in the quantity of real money balances.

Real Cost Approach to International Trade. The Ricardian theory of comparative advantage has been based on a real cost approach. Real cost was initially the exertion of labour in making a commodity, but it got subsequently extended to the use of capital, because the formation of capital involves abstinence from present consumption. The approach maintains that it is in differences in real costs which comparative advantage lies.

Real Gross National Product. Refers to the value of the output of the national economy which is measured in the prices of some base year, allowing a true measure of the change in actual economic physical output.

Real Income. The term used for the value of goods and services produced within a given time period. The changes in real income over or between time periods have been computed by adjusting changes in nominal income arising from changes in the level of prices alone.

Real Interest Rate. An interest rate which is calculated by deflating nominal interest rate by the rate of inflation.

Realized Profit. Refers to the sum of Current Operating Profit and realized Holding Gains.

Real Money Balances. Means the quantity of goods and services which could be purchased from a given stock of money held by individuals.

Real Proprietary Capital. Refers to the value of the net assets of an enterprise in units of general purchasing power, as in Current Purchasing Power (CPP), Accounting and Relative Price Change Accounting.

Realty. Immovable property like land, in contradistinction to Personalty or movable property.

Real Wages. Wage rates or wage earnings which could be measured in terms of the goods and services they can buy.

Receiver. A person appointed usually by a bank or the trustees for debenture holders, to take possession of those assets of a company covered by a Floating Charge and to realize sufficient of them to repay the principal and accrued interest, and to pay all liabilities ranking before the debentures, plus the costs of the receivership and the receiver's remuneration.

Receiving Order. An order by which the court declares a debtor or debtors bankrupt and vests the assets in the Official Receiver.

Recession. Means a significant reduction in employment and production, trade and investment.

Reciprocal Demand. Refers to the demand by one country, in terms of its own goods offered, for the goods of another. The concept was given by J.S. Mill.

Recognition Lag. Means the period that elapses between the time an economic disturbance takes place and the time policy-makers and governments recognise that action is needed.

Reconstruction. Refers to a change in the Capital Structure of a Company, including schemes for the Amalgamation of two or more companies.

Recontract. Refers to an arrangement by which buyers or sellers are able to change the amount on offer if that particular set of prices does not clear the market, the amounts will then get changed according to whether there is an excess-demand or excess-supply situation.

Recoverable Amount. Refers to the greater of the Net Realizable Value (NRV) and Net Present Value (NVP) of an asset.

Recursive Model. It is a model in which the current values of one set of variables could determine the current value of another, whereas previous (or lagged) values of the latter determine the current values of the former.

Recycling. The term used for the practice of returning the waste so that it can be re-used to manufacture the same product as before some other product.

Redeemable Shares. The shares, whether preference or ordinary, which are specifically redeemable under their terms of issue.

Redemption. Refers to the repayment of shares and debentures (stocks and bonds), usually at prearranged amounts and times.

Redemption Yield. Refers to a Yield which takes account not only of periodical returns on an investment but also of the amount receivable on redemption.

Redistribution. The term used for the process of altering the existing distribution of (usually) income or wealth in a society.

Redundenies. Involuntary job losses which occur due to a reduction in manpower requirements on the part of firm.

Re-export. A good which is imported from one country, and is not consumed within the importing country but is instead sent to a third country.

Regional Development Grant. This term used for the payments made by the government to firms which are undertaking new manufacturing investment in those regions designated as Development Areas and Special Development Areas.

Regional Economics. That branch of economic analysis which deals with the spatial distribution of economic activity and spatial variation in levels of economic performance. The subject could be split in the usual way into macroeconomic and microeconomic topics.

Regional Policy. Refers to a form of government economic policy which has been aimed at altering the regional pattern of economic activity or economic performance.

Register of Charges. A Statutory Book kept by companies. It contains details of all charges created by the company upon its assets (including fixed and floating charges to secured debentures) and required to be registered with the Registrar of Companies.

Register of Members. A Statutory Book required to be kept by companies limited by shares, containing the member's (i.e., shareholders') names and addresses, numbers of shares held, with serial numbers if any, amounts paid or deemed to be paid, and dates of entry on the register and of ceasing to be a member. The register of members is usually combined in practice with a Share Ledger.

Registrar of Companies. The government officer with whom Annual Reports including financial statements and other documents must be filed.

Registration Statement. A formal statement, required to be filed with the Securities and Exchange Commission or other body. It contains financial and other information relating to a proposed sale of securities.

Regressand. Refers to the dependent variable in a regression analysis.

Regressive Tax. Normally the term is used to refer to a situation where the rate of tax falls as income rises. Most indirect taxes are generally considered to be regressive.

Regressive Tax. A tax that takes a decreasing proportion of a taxpayer's income, (or other tax base) as his income rises.

Regressor. An independent variable in a regression analysis.

Regulation of Corporate Financial Reporting. The establishment and enforcement of the rules to be followed by companies in their published financial statements.

Related Company. A company, other than a Group Company, in which an investing company holds, on a long-term basis, a qualifying capital interest (usually 20% or more of equity share capital carrying voting rights) for the purpose of securing a contribution to the investing company's own activities by the exercise of any control or influence arising from that interest.

Relative Income Hypothesis. According to this hypothesis, individual and/or household consumption has been a function both of income relative to that of other households or individual and to the level of income in the immediately preceding periods.

Relative Price Change Accounting. Forms of Inflation Accounting that take account of changes in both the General Price Level and in Specific Prices.

Relative Price Changes. Changes in the prices of specific goods and services relative to each other, independent of changes in the General Price Level.

Relevant Range. Refers to that range of activity over which budgeted sales and expense relationship (frequently assumed to be linear) remain valid.

Reliability. A desirable qualitative characteristic of accounting information.

Renewable Resource. The term used for any resource which is capable of being replenished, in part or whole, by 'natural' means Examples include fish, timber, animal populations.

Rent. Economic Rent.

Rent Gradient. A relationship used in urban economics. It expresses the rent paid for use of a unit of land as a function of distance from some reference point—generally the city or town centre.

Rentiers. Owners of capital who derive all or most of their income from this source, but who choose to exert no effective control over its use.

Rent, Ricardo's Theory of. It is a proposition which states that the rent of a piece of land has been the excess of the yield of that piece of land over that of the worst land in cultivation. Ricardo regarded that land at the margin of cultivation yielded no rent, indeed if rent was charged the land would not be cultivated. Farmers would have to pay more for the use of more fertile land, and the excess yield over that of 'no-rent' land would be its rent. Hence the net return to farmers on a unit of land of any given fertility would tend to be the same. Recardo regarded the rent of land as a surplus or economic rent.

Replacement Cost. The cost of replacing an asset. Replacement cost can be interpreted as either the cost of reproduction (i.e., replacement cost of the physical object) or the cost of equivalent services.

Replacement of Cost Accounting. The term used for a method of accounting which adjusts for price changes by calculating profit as the difference between the selling price of a good and its replacement cost on date of sale.

Replacement Investment. Means the amount necessary for replacing that part of the capital stock which has been used up in the process of production.

Replacement Ratio. Refers to the ratio of total net resources (income plus benefits net of tax and housing outlays, allowing for rent and rate rebates) when unemployed to that when working.

Representative Firm. A firm which is characteristic of the industry or sector of the economy being analysed.

Repressed Inflation. Refers to a situation where a price freeze has been controlling the rate of change of prices without affecting the underlying inflationary tendencies.

Reproduction Cost. Costs which are involved to achieve a sustained level of production, such costs might be involved in conserving the natural environment or offering a training programme for recruits to the industry.

Required Rate of Return. The rate of return required by an enterprise on its capital investment projects.

Resale Price Maintenance. A trade practice which binds shopkeepers and dealers to sell goods at prices laid down by the manufacturer or other supplier.

Reserve Accounting. Refers to the practice of passing extraordinary and prior year items through reserves rather than through the profit and loss account.

Reserve Base. The term used for the quantity in the financial system of those assets which, either practically or legally, may constitute the reserves of the banking system, and which in the traditional theory of the credit multiplier from the multiplicand on which that multiplier operates to find out the total quantity of bank deposit money.

Reserve Bank of India. Prior to the establishment of the Reserve Bank of India in 1935, the Imperial Bank of India, though primarily a commercial bank, carried out certain central banking functions and in particular acted as a banker to the Government.

The main function of the Bank has been to regulate the issue of bank notes and keep reserves for securing monetary stability. The Bank is the sole authority for the issue of currency in India other than one rupee coins/notes and subsidiary coins. As the agent of the Central Government, it undertakes the distribution of one rupee notes and coins as well as small coins issued by the Government of India.

The Bank acts as banker to the Government of India, State governments, commercial banks and to some of the financial institutions including state co-operative banks. It formulates and administers monetary policy in order to influence the level of aggregate demand for goods and services by varying the cost and availability of credit. The Reserve Bank also plays vital role in the maintenance of the exchange value of the rupee, and acts as an agent of the government in respect of India's membership of the International Monetary Fund. The Bank also undertakes a variety of developmental and promotional functions.

Reserve Currency. The name assigned to a foreign currency which a government is prepared to hold as parts of its foreign exchange reserves. It is used to finance international trade.

Reserve-deposit Ratio. Refers to the ratio of reserves which are to be held with the Reserve Bank of certain countries by the commercial banks and the deposits held by the banks.

Reserve Fund. In company accounting, a Reserve represented by an earmarked asset (usually cash or investiments).

Reserve Liability. An amount outstanding on a partly paid share that by special resolution of the company cannot be called up except on a winding-up.

Reserve Requirements. Refers to the volume of reserves that member banks must hold with a central bank of certain country as a percentage against existing deposits.

Reserves. In company accounting, those items of Owners Equity that arise from Share Premiums, the retention of profits and the upward revaluation of assets. Reserves should not be confused with Provisions.

Reserve Tranche. Formerly termed as the gold tranche. It is a credit line extended by the International Monetary Fund. The reserve tranche is 25 per cent of a country's quota and may be borrowed automatically. In addition to the reserve tranche, there have been three credit tranches (each being 25 per cent of the quota) carrying progressively tougther terms.

Residual Equity. Refers to that group of claimants in a company whose rights are superseded by all other claimants (normally the ordinary shareholders or common stockholders).

Residual Income. Refers to the net income of an Investment Centre, less the imputed interest on the net assets invested in the centre. It can be used as an alternative measure of the performance of the centre to Return on Investment (ROI).

Residual Value. Refers to the value, actual or estimated, of a fixed asset at the end of its economic life. In practice it is often assumed to be zero.

Responsibility Accounting. Refers to a system of accounting in which Responsibility Centres are established throughout an organization and individual managers are held responsible for costs (Cost Centres), revenues and costs (Profit Centres) or revenues costs and investments (Investment Centres).

Restrictive Practice. (a)Any inefficient working method or system which has been difficult to alter, due to opposition from the management, the workers or both.

(b) Also, refers to a practice in restraint of trade or production. Among firms such practices as common prices, collusive tendering, allotment of sales or output quotas, division of markets, exclusive dealing and loyalty rebates to customers may be used.

Retail. The term used for the final stage in the chain of distribution from manufacturer to consumer. It is the outlet for goods and services purchased by consumers.

Retail Banking. The term is applicable to the traditional banking operations which are being conducted by the clearing banks and increasingly by the trustee savings banks and others, through their branch systems, with the general public.

Retail Price Index. An index number of prices of goods which has been often referred to as the 'cost of living index'. It is regarded as a measure of relative changes in the prices of a specified set of consumer goods which would be bought by the average household on a regular basis.

Retained Profits. Profits not distributed to shareholders but reinvested in a company.

Retention Ratio. Refers to the percentage of the available disposable income (i.e., earnings after tax and after fixed interest and dividend obligations have been met) retained within the firm.

Retentions. The name assigned to retained earnings or undistributed profits.

Return on Investment (ROI). The relationship between profit and investment, used as a measure of performance of an Investment Centre (which may be a division, a company or a group of companies). Return on investment can be analysed as follows:

$$\frac{\text{Sales}}{\text{investment}} \times \frac{\text{profit}}{\text{sales}} = \frac{\text{profit}}{\text{investment}}$$

Returns Inwards. Sales returns, i.e., goods sold but then returned by one enterprise to another.

Returns Outwards. Purchases returns, i.e., goods purchased but then returned by one enterprise to another.

Returns to Scale. Refers to the rate at which output changes as the quantities of all inputs are varied.

Resource Rent Tax. A tax which is based on profits in excess of a level necessary for the commencement or continuation of a project.

Revaluation. Refers to the writing-up of a fixed asset to its current market value.

Revaluation Account. An account used in Partnership Accounts when assets are revalued on the admission, death or retirement of a partner.

Revealed Preference Theory (R.P.T.). First formulated by Professor Paul A. Samuelson (b. 1915). It is a theory of consumer behaviour based solely on an analysis of choices actually made by the consumer in various price-income situations. A given income level and set of prices makes the consumer to select 'bundles' of goods he could purchase; the bundle selected is the revealed preference to all the other bundles that might have been purchased instead. Another income-price situation could reveal another bundle of goods as the revealed preference.

Revenue Account. Refers to the equivalent of a profit and loss account or income and expenditure account in public sector accounting.

Revenue Expenditure. Expenditure that is written off completely in the profit and loss account in the accounting period in which it is made.

Revenue Recognition. Recognizing and recording revenue in the accounts.

Revenue Reserve. In company accounting, any Reserve that is not a Capital Reserve.

Reverse Dumping. Refers to the practice of selling a good abroad at a price higher than that charged for the same good in the domestic market to take advantage of a monopoly position.

Revolving Credit Agreement. A written contractual agreement which is made between a commercial bank and a customer for the bank to offer short-term funds up to a specified limit for a stipulated period of time at an interest rate generally tied to the prime rate.

Inflation: The economic situation in a country, of steadily rising prices, resulting in the diminution of purchasing power of money. Excessive amount of inflation is called galloping inflation of hyper-inflation Cost-push inflation is caused by rise in the cost of production, especially because of wage increases. Demand-pull inflation is caused by excessive increase in money supply without a maching increase in production.

Stagflation: The situation in which stagnation and inflation exist side by side.

Recession: Reduction in production and employment over a short period for want of sufficient demand for goods.

Depression: That State of economy in which men and machinery remain idle over a long period for want of sufficient demand.

Deflation: A reduction in the level of economic activity in the economy as a result of failing prices apprecsiation in the value of money.

Disinflationary measure: Step taken by the government to bring down prices when inflation is chronic.

Reflation. The State of recovery from recession or depression, caused by introduction of spending measures by the government.

Right Issue. Refers to an issue of shares in which the existing shareholders have a pre-emptive right to subscribe for the new shares. The offer price is usually, fixed a little below the current market price.

Risk. Refers to a situation in which future events are not known with certainty but an array of alternative outcomes and their probabilities can be estimated.

Risk Aversion. A tendency to avoid risk. A risk averter is a person with a diminishing Marginal Utility of money who requires a higher expected return as compensation for an increase in risk.

Risk Capital. Capital subject to considerable risk. It is also called 'venture capital'.

Risk Congruence. Sharing of the same attitudes towards risk on the part of superiors and their subordinates.

Risk Management. The term deals with the process of identification, classification, measurement, and appropriate control of risks that threaten assets, both people and property, and the prospective earnings of a business or other enterprise.

Risk Premium. 1. An addition to the 'pure' discount rate so as to take account of the uncertainty associated with the future benefits or revenue from a project.

2. In an uncertain world, refers to that part of the return to capital which compensates the owners of capital for the risk involved in its use in business ventures.

Rival. If one individual's consumption of a good reduces the quantity available to others then that good is considered to display rivalness or to be rival in consumption.

Roll Over Relief. A tax relief that allows a capital gain realized on the sale of a fixed asset to be deducted for tax purposes from the cost of the replacements asset.

RPI. Abbreviation of Retail Price Index.

Rule-of-thumb. A simple formula or procedure which forms the basis for decision-making by economic agents. It can be argued that under conditions of imperfect information and uncertainty resort to rough and ready rules has been unavoidable.

S

Salary. The term used for the remuneration of almost all nonmanual and some manual employees in exchange for the supply of labour services.

Sale and Leaseback. Refers to a transaction in which an owner sells an asset and immediately reacquires the right to use the asset by entering into a lease with the purchaser.

Sales Forecast. Refers to a forecast of future sales which is based on consideration of such factors as past sales volumes, general economic and industry conditions, relationship of the organization's sales to macroeconomic indicators, relative product profitability, market research studies, pricing policies, advertising, quality of the sales force, competition, seasonal variations and productive capacity.

Sales Journal. A book or other record having a chronological list of credit sales. Each entry in the journal is debited to an account in the Debtors Ledger.

Sales Ledger. Synonym for Debtors Ledger.

Sales Tax. A tax which is levied on a market transaction. There have been many types of sales taxes but they may be divided between those which apply to a large range of expenditure and those which apply to the sale of a specific good or service. Thus a value-added tax, a retail sales tax, a turnover tax and a comprehensive expenditure tax have been examples of general sales taxes. Customs, excise and protective duties have been examples of taxes on specific goods.

Salvage Value. Synonym for the Residual Value of a fixed asset.

Samuelson Test. According to the test one situation has been potentially superior in welfare terms to another if for every distribution of the commodity bundle in the first situation there exists some distribution of the second commodity bundle in which at least one person has been better-off and nobody is worse-off. This implies that the point utility possibility curve for the second bundle lies entirely outwith that of the first.

Satisficing. Achieving a satisfactory level of, say, wealth or profits, instead of maximizing.

Saving. That part of income which is not consumed; the withholding of money from expenditure on goods and services. In discussing the national economy, however, economists frequently use the term 'saving' for expenditure of a special kind—the employment of income in the creation of new capital.

Saving Banks. Institutions which are aiming at encouraging and facilitating the small saver.

Savings Equal Investment. Refers to a maximum of Lord Keynes (1884-1946) who defined savings and expenditure on capital goods or investment as being of necessity equal to one another.

Say's Law of Markets. A law which was formulated by the French economist J.B. Say. This law states that every increase in the supply of goods is a corresponding increase in the demand for goods so long as producers have directed their production in accordance with each other's wants.

Scarcity. In economics, this term is usually reserved for situations in which the resources available for producing output have been insufficient to satisfy wants.

Scarce Currency. Another name for hard currency.

Scorekeeping. Refers to the accounting function of accumulating data and reporting to all levels of management.

Scrap. Residue from a manufacturing process which can be either sold or re-used. It has a small but measurable value.

S rap Value. Synonym for the Residual Value of a fixed asset.

S rip. A popular term for share and bond certificates.

S.ripophily. Refers to the collection and study of Share Certificates and bond certificates.

Secondary Industry or Manufacturing Industry. Refers to the processing of raw materials into finished products, including such activities as building and construction, and the supply of electricity and gas.

Secondary Market. It is a market for the resale and purchase of securities or other titles to property or commodities outside the organized exchange or primary markets.

Secret Reserves. Undisclosed understatement of net worth resulting from, e.g., the excessive writing down of assets, overstatement of provisions and liabilities, and the writing off of additions to fixed assets as expenses.

Securities. A loose term which is embracing a wide range of financial assets, e.g., gilt-edged stock, equities and debentures. Short-term assets like bills have been sometimes included, but the word tends to refer to longer-term assets. Securities are in two main forms:

(a) bonds, fully-paid stock, shares, stock units and unnumbered shares; and

(b) partly-paid stock or shares.

Security Capital. Capital which is subject to a minimum amount of risk, as opposed to risk or venture capital.

Security Market Line. Refers to the linear relationship between the expected return of a security and its Systematic Risk, the expected return comprising a risk-free return plus a risk premium.

Segment Reporting. Refers to the reporting to outsiders of the results of a diversified group of companies by major class of business and geographical area.

Selective Credit Control. Control of credit to certain sectors of the economy or for particular purposes of borrowing.

Self-assessment. A system under which the taxpayer rather than the tax authority is primarily responsible for calculating tax liability and ensuring that payment is made.

Self-balancing Ledgers. Ledgers that contain an equal amount of debits and credits. This should always be true of the General Ledger and is also true of those Subsidiary Ledgers that contain general ledger control accounts.

Self-liquidating Advances. Bank advances to customers which are for the purpose of trading over a temporary shortage of funds only e.g. when the farmer is faced with a heavy outlay of wages during the 'seed-time' to harvest period, the load being repaid when the crop is sold.

Seller's Market. Market dominated by sellers. The sellers dictate prices because of too much demand and in adequate supply.

Selling Hedge or Short Hedge. Selling futures contracts to provide protection against a possible decline in the prices of commodities.

Semivariable Cost. A cost that has both fixed and variable elements. Some services, for example, are paid for by a minimum charge plus a variable cost based on use.

Sensitivity Analysis. Varying the data in a calculation so as to ascertain which variables have a material effect on the results.

Separable Costs. Cost incurred beyond the Split Off Point for Joint Products.

Service of Debt. Refers to the payment of the interest due to on a debt.

Services. In an economic sense, they may be defined as any functions or tasks that are performed, for which there is has been a demand and hence a price determined in the relevant market. They are sometimes referred to as intangible goods.

Settlement Day. A synonym for Account Day.

Shadow Price. Refers to the Opportunity Cost of a scarce resource, i.e., a shadow price is a measure of the Contribution foregone by failing to have one more unit of scarce capacity in a particular situation.

Shadow Wage Rate. Refers to shadow price of labour.

Share. An expression of a proprietary relationship in a company. Shareholders are proportionate owners of a company but the company's net assets belong not to them but to the company as a separate and independent legal entity. The most common types of shares are Ordinary Shares and Preference Shares.

Share Capital. Part of the Owners Equity section of a balance sheet. It does not include the share premium and other Capital Reserves.

Share Certificate. A certificate which is giving documentary evidence of title to a share.

Share Ledger. Refers to a book or other record showing in debit and credit form changes in the shareholding of each member (shareholder) of a company listed by a shares.

Share Premium Account. An account to which is credited the premium on shares issued at a premium. A share premium is treated almost but not quite as if it were share capital.

Shift-share Analysis. A technique which is employed in the analysis of regional economic growth. This attempts to separate out that part of a region's growth which can be 'explained' by the mix of industries in the region (its industrial structure) and that part which is to be explained in terms of particularly 'regional' influences.

Short Banking. The practice of not paying all monies received in business activities into the company's bank account.

Short End of the Treasury Security Market. A reference to short-term Treasury bills and notes with a duration of 90 days, 6 months, and up to 1 year, compared with notes and bonds with a duration in maturity of up to 30 years.

Short Run. Refers to the time period in the production process during which the fixed factors of production cannot get changed, but the level of utilization of variable factors can get altered.

Short-term Money Market. Refers to a market in which large borrowers and lenders of money and large buyers and sellers of securities come together to transact their daily business dealings.

Side Payments. Those exchange between individuals in a group made so as to induce allegiance to some common goals.

Sight Deposits. Refers to deposits held in banks and similar deposit taking institutions which could be transferable by cheque or withdrawable in cash without notice.

Simple Discount. The deduction from the maturity value (S) of an obligation that is sold or settled for an amount P before its maturity date. The amount of the simple discount is S-P,

$$S = P (I + ni) \text{ and } P = S (I - nd),$$

n being the number of periods, i the simple interest rate and d the simple discount rate (d = Pi/S).

Simple Interest. Interest calculated on the original sum (principal) invested and not also on interest reinvested. It can be calculated from the formula I = Pni, where I = the amount of simple interest, P = the principal, n = the number of periods, and i = the simple rate of interest per period.

Simplified Financial Statements. Financial statements with a reduced information content prepared so that those unskilled in accounting (e.g., Naive Investors) may more readily understand a company's financial position and performance.

Single Entry Book-keeping. Refers to a system of bookkeeping which records one aspect only of each transaction. For example, accounts may be kept recording transactions affecting Personal Accounts but not Real Accounts or Nominal Accounts. In practice cash transactions are also likely to be recorded in such a system, i.e., there will be a Cash Book as well as a Personal Ledger. These strictly constitute Incomplete Records rather than single entry accounting.

Sinking Fund. A fund into which the government periodically makes payments in order to accumulate money to clear foreign debts.

Sinner's Taxes. Taxes on alcohol, tobacco and betting.

Site Value Rating. The levying of local rates on owners of land rather than occupiers.

Skewness. Refers to a measure of the lack of symmetry of a statistical distribution. Distributions skewed to the right are positively skewed; distributions skewed to the left are negatively skewed.

Slab Rates of Lending. Two or more interest rates, charged on the amount of loan given to a party. An ordinary rate up to a ceiling and a penal rate beyond it.

Slump. Refers to a severe downturn phase or recession in the trade cycle. Any contractionary phase of the trade cycle could be termed as a slump but the term has been usually reserved for the most severe cases.

Snob-Effect. The effect whereby as the price of a good falls and some sections of the community expand their demand for the good other sections or individuals reduce their demand in order to differentiate themselves from the general trend.

Social Accounting. A synonym for either Social Responsibility Reporting or for National Accounting.

Social Audit. An examination of the extent to which the operations of an organization, public or private, have contributed to social goals. Social audits can be seen as a means of giving some control to groups such as employees, consumers and the local community.

Social Benefits. Benefits, not recorded in the accounts of business enterprises, which arise from the existence of Externalities.

Social Costs. Costs, not recorded in the account of business enterprises, which arise from the existence of Externalities.

Social Economics. Refers to the application of neo-classical economic theory to social policy. Where term 'social' has been interpreted as widely or as narrowly as the individual author chooses, although, most usually encompass health, education, crime, housing and welfare services.

Socialism. A term which is used to describe the general doctrine that the ownership and control of the means of production—capital and land should be held by the community as a whole and administered in the interests of all.

Social Marginal Productivity Criterion. It states that the total net contributions of a unit of investment to output should be regarded when allocating resources and not simply the part which accrues to private investors.

Social Relations of Production. The term which was used by Marx to define the social relationships between humans, which arise from a particular set of material forces of production.

Social Responsibility Reporting. Reporting the costs and benefits relating to socially responsible actions by business enterprises.

Social Returns to Education. Refers to the excess return on education over and above any extra earnings obtained from being educated.

Soft Commodities. Commodities such as coffee, Cocoa, sugar and tea; hence the term 'soft commodities futures markets'.

Soft Company. A company which is engaged in analysis and consultancy, as distinct from the actual development, production and marketing of a range of products.

Soft Currency. A currency which is having a falling exchange rate due to continuing balance of payments deficits.

Soft Loan. A loan which carries easy terms such as low rate of interest, grace period for repayment, and recycling of debt.

Sold Ledger. Synonym for Debtors Ledger.

Sole Proprietor. Refers to the commonest type of business unit in which a single person has been responsible for raising the capital, organising and managing the business, and undertaking the risk.

Sole Trader's Accounts. The accounts and financial statements of an unincorporated enterprise owned by a single person.

Solvency. The ability of a debtor (whether an individual or a corporate body) to pay debts as they fall due.

Sophisticated Investor. An investor with a good knowledge and understanding of the accounting practices and theories relevant to published financial statements or with access to the advice of a person with such knowledge and understanding.

Spatial Monopoly. Refers to an element of monopoly power which is obtained by a retailer or producer through locating at a distance from his competitors.

Spatial Price Discrimination. The term used for a pricing strategy in which firms selling to consumers located at various distances from the producers do not charge each consumer a price for a good equal to the sum of the price of the good 'at the factory gate' (the f.o.b. price) and the true transfer corts of delivering the good.

Special Drawing Rights (S.D.Rs.). An international reserve currency system which was created by the International Monetary Fund in October, 1969. It provides for a new type of money (known as 'paper gold') to serve by agreement of the free world nations as the first international legal tender. S.D.Rs. are used along with gold and dollars as monetary reserves; they are not held by individuals or private businesses but used in transactions between governments and central banks.

Specie. Precious metal in coined form.

Specie Points. Refer to those levels of the exchange rate of a currency which is on a gold standard at which it becomes profitable to move gold into or out of the country.

Specific Price. The prices, observable in a market, of specific goods and services (commodities). A change in a specific price can be divided into two components: that part which is due to a change in the General Price Level; and that part which is due to a change in the price of specific commodities relative to other commodities.

Specific Risk. Synonym for Non-Systematic Risk.

Specific Tax. Generally, a tax which is imposed on each unit of output of a good and not on the value of output.

Speculation. Refers to the practice of buying or selling with the motive of then selling or buying and thereby making a profit if prices or exchange rates have changed.

Speculative Boom. Refers to investment in highly risky projects but with high expected rates of return or capital gain in a period of rapid economic expansion or boom.

Speculative Demand. Refers to the demand for money for the purchase of financial assets, as distinct from the transactions demand for money.

Split-rate System. A system of taxation in which a lower rate of tax is charged on distributed income than on undistributed income.

Spoilage. Goods that are not up to standard and are sold for disposal value.

Spread Effects. Beneficial effects of the growth of a regional economy on the economies of other regions.

Stability. Refers to the extent to which an equilibrium price or set of prices will be secured despite any 'shocks' to the system which temporarily move price away from its equilibrium level.

Stabilization Function. Refers to the role of government in manipulating fiscal and monetary policies for the purpose of maintaining a high and even level of economic activity.

Stabilized Accounting. The stabilization of financial statements drawn up in nominal monetary units by the substitution as the unit of account of gold (as in the German hyper-inflation of the 1920s) or a measure of general purchasing power.

Stag. An investor who makes an application for a new security in the hope that on Allotment it can be sold at a premium over the issue price.

Stagflation. The terms for the periods of recession and rising unemployment coupled with positive rates of price inflation.

Stakeholders. Individual interests associated with an accounting entity and in some degree dependent upon its financial performance.

Standard Commodity. It is a composite commodity which is constructed such that its price does not change when there are changes in the distribution of income.

Standard Costing. A system of costing using Standard Costs. The major purpose of a standard costing system is improved control over operations but it may also be used to save record-keeping costs.

Standard Costs. Predetermined measures of what costs should be under specified conditions.

Standard of Living. It is also referred to as the level of economic welfare, utility or real income. It refers to the level of material well-being of an individual or household. In economic analysis, the standard of living has been usually held to be determined by the quantities of goods and services (including leisure) consumed.

Standard Setting. Setting the rules to be followed in the preparation of corporate financial statements.

Standard Stream Concepts of Income. Concepts of income based on the maintenance intact of a stream of future receipts (e.g., dividends to shareholders) in real or money terms.

Statement of Affairs. A statement as to the affairs of a company required in windings up and in receiverships.

Static Budget. A Budget based on a single planned volume level.

Stationary State. A state of nature in which all prices are constant through time and are expected to remain so, and in which each asset has a single price (i.e., replacement cost, net realizable and net present value are all equal to each other).

Statutory Audit. An Audit required by statute of the financial statements of limited companies and other organizations.

Statutory Liquidity Ratio. The percentage of the total assets of a scheduled bank which should be maintained in liquid assets, like cash. This ratio is fixed by the RBI in India.

Steady-state Growth. In growth theory it refers to a dynamic condition of an economy where all real variables have been growing at a constant proportional rate (which may be zero or negative).

Sterling Area. It has a group of countries and territories which, because of their strong trade and financial connections with the UK tended to stabilize the exchange rate of their currencies with sterling, and to hold all or a large part of their external reserves in sterling.

Stock. The issued capital of a company, or a particular issue of securities, e.g., by a government, which has been in a consolidated form so that it can be held or transferred in any amounts.

Stock Appreciation. That part of the increase in the monetary value of stock-in-trade (inventories) which is due to changes in prices rather than changes in physical quantities.

Stock Appreciation Relief. A tax relief that aimed to alleviate the taxation of unrealized gains on stocks (inventories) during periods of rising prices.

Stocks. A general term comprising goods or other assets purchased for resale; consumable stores; raw materials and components purchased for incorporation into products for sale; products and services in intermediate stages of completion; and finished goods.

Stock Turnover. The ratio of cost of sales or sales to stock-in-trade (inventory) i.e., sales/stocks or (cost of sales)/stocks.

Stores Ledger Control Account. An account recording in total materials purchased and issued to production and the balance which should be on hand at any given moment.

Straddle Option. A combination of a 'put' option and a 'call' option which may be exercised in both respects at a common specified price before the expiry date.

Stratified Sampling. In an audit context, a method of sampling in which the population is divided into strata, each stratum being subject to a separate test.

Strike Insurance. In some countries it is a form of mutual aid used by a variety of industrial concerns to protect themselves against the selective strike tactic.

Structure of Taxes. Every country is having a range of different types of taxes. The structure of the tax system refers to this mix.

Subdivision of Shares. The division of shares of one nominal value into a larger number of shares of a smaller nominal value.

Subsidiary. A company controlled by a Holding Company. A company is a subsidiary of another company if that other company is a member of it and controls the composition of its board of directors, or if the other company holds more than half the nominal value of its Equity Share Capital.

Subsidiary Ledger. A ledger in which a special class of Accounts (e.g., debtors) is kept so as not to overburden the General Ledger and to allow separate usage.

Subsidy. A payment which is made by the government (or possibly by private individuals) which forms a wedge between the price consumers pay and the costs incurred by producers, such that price has been less than marginal cost.

Subsistence Expenditures. A level of expenditure which is necessary to sustain a subsistence of 'survival' standard of living.

Substance Over Form. An accounting concept whereby transactions or other events are accounted for and presented in accordance with their economic reality rather then their legal form.

Substantive Tests. Auditing tests the purpose of which is to obtain evidence as to the completeness, accuracy and validity of information in accounting records or in financial statements.

Substitute. Means a good which can be substituted for another good, or an input that could be substituted for another input.

Substitution Effect. Refers to the effect on the demand for a good of a change in price of that good assuming real income has been held constant. The meaning of 'real income' varies according to which measure of the substitution effect is chosen.

Super-neutrality. Money is considered to have this property if a change in the rate of growth of the supply of money does not have any effect on the rate of growth of real output in the longrun.

Supernumerary Expenditure. Refers to expenditure on a good or group of goods over and above some minimum or subsistence expenditure.

Sunk Costs. Costs incurred in the past and unaffected by any future action and thus irrelevant to decision-making.

Supplementary Financial Statements. Statements presented as additional to primary financial statements and explicitly or implicitly of less importance.

Supply. Means the amount of a commodity or service which will be offered for sale at a given price per unit of time.

Supply and Demand Curves. A graphical presentation of supply and demand functions, showing on the one hand how much of a commodity will be supplied per unit of time at any given price, and on the other how much of a commodity will be bought per unit of time at any given price.

Supply and Demand, Laws of. In respect of goods and services:

(a) If, at the price ruling, demand exceeds supply, the price tends to rise; conversely, when supply exceeds demand the price tends to fall;

(b) A rise in price tends to contract demand and expand supply; conversely, a fall in price tends to expand demand and to contract supply;

(c) Price tends to a level at which the demand is equal to the supply, i.e., to an 'equilibrium price';

(d) The greater the increase in price, the greater the expansion in supply; and

(e) For any given price increase, the expansion in the quantity supplied will be greater, the longer the time the market is allowed to adjust.

Supply Curve. The term used for a graphical representation of the relationship between the supply of a commodity and its price (usually with price on the vertical axis, and quantity supplied measured along the horizontal axis).

Supply Management. Regulation of supply of a commodity through incentives for production, etc. Both operations are means to control price.

Supply-side Economics. Refers to a body of thought which emphasizes that the principal determinant of the rate of growth of national output in both the short and long-run has been the allocation and efficient use of the labour and capital in an economy.

Support Price. Also known as the floor price, is the minimum guaranteed price for the producers. This is announced by the government in order to encourage production.

Surplus Units. Any economic unit whose assets become grater than its liabilities, and has been therefore willing to lend money, extend credit, or purchase financial instruments.

Swiss Numbered Accounts. Anonymous accounts permitted in the banking system of Switzerland; secrecy is protected not only by civil but also by the criminal law.

Syndicated Loans. Refers to loans which are involving several banks joining together to raise massive sums (say $ 1 billion or more) for a single borrower.

Systematic (Market) Risk. The non-diversifiable component of the risk of a security.

Systematic Random Sampling. In an audit context, a method of drawing a sample in which the first item is chosen at random and then every k^{th} item thereafter is chosen, where k is the number of items in the population divided by the required sample size, until the full sample has been down.

Systems-based Audit. An audit in which the nature and depth of audit tests depends upon the auditor's evaluation of the internal control system and in which that evaluation forms a major part of the audit.

T

T Account. An Account with a left-hand side recording Debit Entries and a right-hand side recording Credit Entries.

Take-over. Means the acquisition by a 'raider' company of more than 51 per cent of the voting shares of another company.

Take-over. Refers to the acquisition by one company of sufficient shares in another company to give the purchaser control of that other company.

Take-over Bid. Refers to an offer by one company to acquire all, or a controlling holding, of the voting shares of another company.

Tangible Assets. The term used for physical assets such as plant and machinery, which are distinguished from intangible assets like as the value of a patent or a firm's goodwill.

Tap Issue. Means the issue of bills and securities by the Treasury direct to Government Departments and other buyers at a special price, without going through the market.

Targets (also known as policy targets). These refer to a set of quantitatively fixed objective of economic policy, to be achieved by a choice of values for policy instruments.

Tariff. (a) It is a duty or tax which is charged by a country on its imports from other countries; a customs duty.

(b) It also refers to a method of charging for services, e.g., supplies of gas or electricity.

Tariff Structure. The term used for the overall pattern of tariff rates. Tariffs are not usually applicable to all imports at a uniform rate.

Taxable Income. For an individual Earned Income plus Investment Income less expenses and allowances; for a company, income as adjusted for items not allowed for tax purposes, for revenues not taxed and for deductions (e.g., Capital Allowances) not in the company's accounts.

Tax Allowances. Deductions from total income making part of that income tax-free regardless of the taxpayer's pattern of expenditure or source of income. The part remaining is the taxable income.

Taxation. Compulsory levies on private individuals and organizations which are made by government to raise revenue to finance expenditure on public goods and services, and to control the volume of private expenditure in the economy. Taxes are classified in various ways. Some are termed as direct taxes, examples of which are income tax and wealth tax. Others have been called indirect taxes. These are taxes on transactions especially expenditure. Examples have been excise duties and value-added tax.

Taxation Adam Smith's, Canons of. Simith's canons of taxation were as follows:

(a) the amounts people paid in taxes should be equal, i.e. proportional to their incomes;

(b) there should be certainty with regard to the amount to be paid;

(c) there should be convenience of payment and collection;

(d) economy should be observed so that taxes should not be imposed of a kind where the cost of collection was excessive.

Tax Avoidance and Evasion. Respectively, manipulation within the law to reduce liability for tax and manipulation outside the law to reduce liability.

Taxes. Refer to compulsory financial contribution by a person or body of persons towards the expenditure of a public authority. Taxes on income (i.e on wages, salaries, profits; dividends, rent and interest) and on capital have been known as 'direct' taxes.

Tax Avoidance Scheme. A business scheme which seeks to avoid or minimise the payment of tax.

Tax Base. Refers to the base on which a tax is levied, e.g., a stock of wealth, a flow of income, an expenditure.

Tax Break. A situation which is providing some relief from tax, in whole or part.

Tax Code. (1) A means of summarizing the amount of allowances and deductions due to a taxpayer, so as to determine his taxable income.

(2) The whole body of tax law, especially in countries where the law is codified rather than existing in statutes and decided cases.

Tax Credit. A credit which is given directly against a tax; the tax payable gets reduced by the amount of the credit. It can apply in several different situations.

Tax Credit Scheme. An income maintenance programme in which everyone has been guaranteed a minimum income, while income above that level is taxed. When a certain income level is reached, the tax paid will be just equal to the guaranteed payment this is the 'break-even' income level.

Taxes. Compulsory levies made by public authorities for which nothing is received directly in return. They are used in part to provide Public Goods. Taxes may be classified in a number of

ways, for example as in the diagram below:

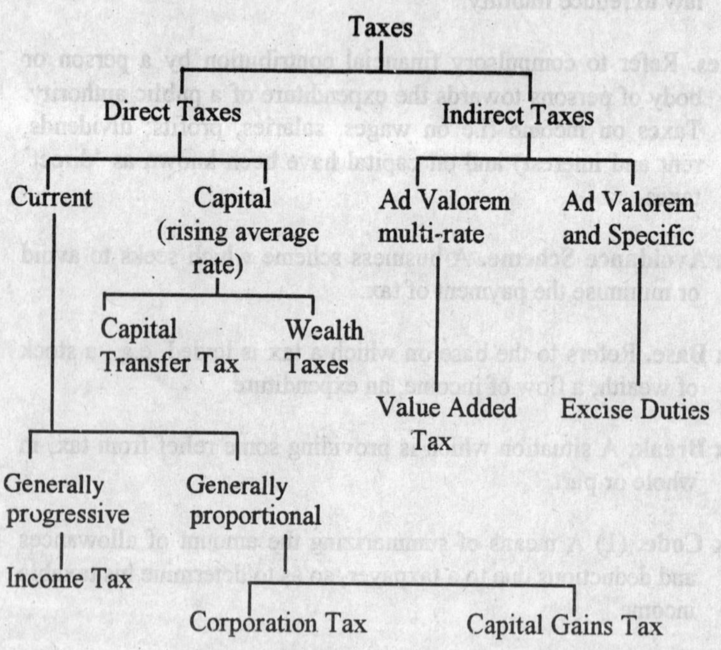

Tax Evasion Scheme. A business scheme which helps to avoid or minimise the payment of tax; it is basically unlawful infringing the framework and principles of existing legislation.

Tax Expenditure. A term which is used to describe the various allowances which may be used to reduce tax liability—generally liability to income tax.

Tax Haven. A place which offers a combination of low taxes, stability and encouragement of free enterprise.

Tax Return. A statement to the fiscal authorities of a taxpayer's sources and totals of income and expenses during a given period.

Tax-rort Account. False bank accounts, which may be opened for the purposes of tax evasion.

Tax Sharing. Proposals that a federal or central government share some part of its tax collections with state and local governments.

Tax Shelter. A medium or process which is intended to reduce or eliminate the tax burden of the individual.

Tax Shifting. Refers to the phenomenon whereby those on whom taxes are levied are able to pass the burden either partly or fully on to others.

Tax Yield. The revenue which is collected from a tax.

Teeming and Lading. The misappropriation of cash remittances received from customers by using amounts from later remittances to fill the gap left by the earlier misappropriation.

Tenders. These are the offers made to supply at a fixed price. A discount house, for example, tendering for an issue of Treasury Bills, will offer to take up so many bills at a certain price.

Tender to Contract Cover (T.T.C.). Refers to an option which allows exporters to fix forward exchange rates on which to base their tender prices.

Term Assurance. Refers to a form of insurance life cover; the life office agrees to insure the policyholder's life for a fixed term for a fixed annual premium; if the policyholder outlives the term of the policy, nothing a payable.

Term Loan. A bank loan made for a fixed term of years, at a fixed rate of interest, and normally repayable by instalments spread over a period.

Terms of Trade. The term used for the relationship between the prices of exports and imports. It may be expressed as an index:

$$\text{Index of Terms of Trade} = \frac{\text{Price Index of Exports}}{\text{Price Index of Imports}}$$

Tertiary Industry. Means the provision of a wide range of services which are required by the primary and secondary industries and by individual consumers, e.g., the provision of transport and communication; commercial and financial services such as insurance and banking; the provision of health, legal and educational services; and the wholesale and retail trade.

Test Deck. In an audit context, a set of simulated transactions that the auditor can put through a computer system in order to see whether they are processed accurately.

Threshold Effect. Means an increase in the level of taxation which a community is said to be willing to pay resulting from some crisis or national emergency.

Threshold of a Good. In regional or spatial economics, it refers to the minimum population which can provide a market for some good or service.

Thifts. Financial institutions such as savings and loans associations, mutual savings banks, and credit unions.

Throughput Economy. Type of an economy in which resources are continuously set up without replacement or recycling.

Tight Money. A monetary policy which is regarded as retarding economic activity. Opposite of easy money.

Times Deposit. Means an interest-bearing deposit for a fixed period of time.

Time Interest Earned. Refers to the number of times that a company's interest charges are covered by its earnings before interest and tax (EBIT).

Time Sharing. Refers to an arrangement in which the financial contribution towards the purchase of an asset has been related to the use of that asset in terms of time, thus a group of purchasers may share the cost of a 'second home', each enjoying the right to occupy it for a prescribed period of the year.

Time Value of Money. An expression of the fact that, if the rate of interest is positive, money in hand now is worth more than money to be received at a date in future.

Timing Differences. Differences, capable of being reversed in future periods, between profits as computed for taxation purposes and profits as stated in financial statements.

Token Money. Refers to any form of money the value of which as means of payment rests on legal enactment.

Total Cost. Refers to the total cost of producing are given level of output. In the short-run total costs could be divided into two parts, fixed costs, i.e., those costs which do not vary with output (sometimes referred to as overhead costs), and variable costs, i.e., those costs which vary directly with output.

Total Revenue. Refers to the total receipts from sales of a product or series of products produced by a single firm or industry.

Trade. Means the exchange of commodities between individuals or groups either directly through barter or indirectly through a medium such as money.

Trade Barrier. This is a general term to cover any government limitation on the free international exchange of merchandise. These barriers may take the form of tariffs, quotas, import deposits, restrictions on the grant of import licences or strict regulations pertaining to health and/or safety standards.

Trade Bill. A commercial bill which is used in transactions actually involving goods. A trade bill has been drawn by the seller and accepted by the buyer, and has been payable on a set date in respect of goods purchased.

Trade Credit. Credit which is extended by a trader or producer to his customers through terms of sale which permit payment at some time after the actual transfer of the goods.

Trade Cycle. Alternating periods of trade boom and depression, especially characteristic of 19th century business activity when cycles of this nature occurred at fairly regular intervals.

Trade Cycle, Theories of The. Theories adduced by economists to explain fluctuations in trade have included:

(a) 'Real causes' theories, (i) Attempts to explain the trade cycle in terms of harvest fluctuations attributable to the weather. One of the most famous of these theories was the 'sunspot' theory of

William Stanley Jevons (1835-1882).

(b) Psychological theories: Theories that business persons are influenced alternately by waves of optimism and pessimism. When trade is good people are optimistic, buying more while prices rise and production is stimulated. When trade is poor pessimism prevails buying is reduced prices fall and production is depressed.

(c) Monetary theories: Theories that stress the role of the quantity of money and credit, and the rate of interest, in influencing business activity. The view that the trade cycle is a purely monetary phenomenon has been held by Ralph G. Hawtrey (1879-1975) who regarded the Bank Rate as the mainspring of cyclical change.

(d) Over-production and under-consumption theories: Numerous and diverse theories but all may be described as theories of the deficiency of effective demand. John A. Hobson (1858-1940) argued that in good times profits increase without a corresponding increase in the wages level and the purchasing power in the hands of the general public. Surplus profits are invested and productive capacity is greatly enlarged; but there is no market to carry off the increased supply of consumers' goods and a crisis persists until the surplus of stocks is worked off.

(e) Saving-investment theory: A theory that consumption depends on the level of income, and that this in turn depends on real investment. Now saving, i.e., the abstention from the purchase of consumers' goods, is a prerequisite for investment. Thus saving, consumption and investment depend on one another, together determining the level of total income.

Trade. An individual who buys and sells for his own account on an Exchange for short-term profit, also an employee of a broker or financial institution who specialises in handling purchases and sales of securities for the firm or its clients.

Trade Discount. A discount off the list price of a good. Trade discounts are not usually recorded in the accounts.

Trade Mark. A distinctive identification, protected by law, of a manufactured product or service. Trade marks are Intangible

Assets.

Trade Unions. Combinations of workers which are formed for the purpose of taking collective, as distinct from individual, action against their employers for the improvement of pay and other working conditions.

Trading Account. An account showing an enterprise's sales, cost of sales and gross profit.

Trading on the Equity. Using fixed interest sources of capital to boost the rate of return on the Equity.

Transaction. In an accounting context, this term refers to an Event giving rise to a change affecting the operations or financial status of an accounting entity.

Transaction Costs. Refer to those costs other than price which have been incurred in trading goods and services.

Transactions Demand. Means the demand for money that people require to have available for spending, as distinct from the speculative demand for money.

Transactions Demand for Money. Refers to a motive for demanding money for the purpose of transactions, i.e., of payments and receipts, using money in its function as a medium of exchange.

Transfer Incomes. Incomes which cannot be considered as payment for current services to production and which therefore do not enter national income.

Transfer Payments. Payments made by public authorities which are not made in consideration of goods and service currently produced.

Transfer Pricing. The pricing of goods and services which are merely being transferred from one part to another part of the same organisation.

Transformation Problem. Refers to the problem in Marxian economies of deriving a unique set of prices from values, i.e., labour inputs.

Transitory Consumption. Refers to an unanticipated rise or fall in consumption.

Transitory Income. Unanticipated income. A windfall gain or windfall loss.

Treasurership. Refers to the provision to an enterprise of some or all of the following functions: capital-raising, investor relations, short-term financing, banking, custody of assets, the granting of credit, the collection of debts, investment policy, insurance.

Treasury Stock. The stock or shares issued by a company but later reacquired with the intention of reissue. Such shares are not entitled to dividends or votes.

Treasury Bond Tender. The term used for a method of sale of government treasury bonds, adopted by some governments. A tender usually makes provision for two types of bidders—"competitive' and 'non-competitive'.

Trend (also known as Time Trend) 1. An undelying, long-run component in time-series data, which is often calculated to display the long-run direction of movement of a variable.

2. A measure of the average level of an economic magnitude (such as income) at a particular point in time. Cycles may occur around the trend level, which may not be a constant but may grow at a variable or a constant rate.

Trial Balance. A statement which lists the debit and credit ledger balances produced by a double entry recording system at a particular date. The totals of the debit and credit columns should agree but may not do so if errors have been made.

Trust. Refers to various legally defined and regulated arrangements under which assets belonging to an individual or a group are placed in the custody of trustees who, depending on the type of trust, may actually manage them for the benefit of the owners.

Turning Point. Refers to the point in the business cycle when an expansionary phase of the business cycle is replaced by a contractionary phase or vice-versa.

Turnover. A synonym for sales and the word used for sales in the Profit and Loss Account Formats.

Turnpike Theorems. A class of propositions in growth theory which is concerned with the closeness of optimal growth paths to balanced growth at the highest rate. The name 'turnpike theorem' was given by R. Dorfman, P. Samuelson and R. Solow in Linear Programming and Economic Analysis.

Two Sector Growth Model. A model which is used in growth theory where the fundamental differences between consumption and capital goods have been recognized, with one sector concerned with each of the two goods. Examples include the models of J.E. Meade, and H. Uzawa.

Tying Contract. Refers to a condition of sale needing the buyer of a given product to purchase another (different) product, usually complementary to the first product.

Type I Error. The error of rejecting the Null Hypothesis when it is true.

Type II Error. The error of accepting the Null Hypothesis when it is false.

U

U-form Enterprise. Refers to a company in which decision-making has been centralized around a top board of executives whose functional responsibilities are applied to all company products.

Unamortized Debt Discount. Refers to the portion of debt discount that remains and is to be spread over future fiscal periods. Usually appears as a prepaid expense, if related to a bank loan, or as a deferred charge, if related to a long-term bond issue.

Unanticipated Inflation. Refers to that proportion of the actual level of inflation which people did not expect: actual minus expected inflation.

Unapplied Cash. In municipal accounting, cash not reserved for a specific purpose and available for use within the fund of which it is part.

Unappropriated Budget Surplus. In municipal accounting, this term refers to the excess of the estimated revenues of a fund over the original appropriation for a given period of time.

Unappropriated Earned Surplus. Refers to the part of earned surplus that has not been transferred to a subordinate account or earmarked for a specific propose. Such surplus therefore remains available for distributing in the form of dividends.

Unappropriated Income. An account which is set up for budgetary control to which is credited the excess of income, according to a related and approved expense or earnings budget.

Unappropriated Profit. Refers to the part of the profit of a business not paid out in dividend or allocated to any particular use. It implies authorized acts by directors.

Uncalled Capital. Refers to that portion of the issued share capital of a business, payment of which has not yet been requested by the directors.

Uncollectable Account. Refers to a sum of money owing to a business which cannot be claimed because the debtor is insolvent, etc.

Uncontrollable Costs. Costs that cannot be influenced by a given manager within a given time period. In the very long run there are few costs that cannot be controlled by someone.

Unconvertible Money. The kind of paper money, in the case of which the Government does not bear any responsibility of its conversion into standard coins on demand.

Uncrossed Cheque. Refers to a cheque which has not been crossed, and which can be cashed anywhere.

UNCTAD. Abbreviation of United Nations Conference on Trade and Development.

Undated Stock. Government loans for which there is no stated redemption date, e.g., consols. The holder receives an annual income of a fixed interest rate on the loan. The stock may be dealt in on the market.

Underabsorbed Overhead. A debit balance which results from the use of predetermined overhead rates. Less overhead is charged to production than is actually incurred. In practice underabsorbed overhead is usually written off to cost of goods sold rather than prorated over cost of goods sold, finished goods and work in progress.

Under-Bimetallism. The monetary system of the country, under which both gold coins and silver coins circulate simultaneously, and overvalued metal has a tendency to drive the undervalued metal out of circulation.

Under Bond. Denoting imported goods stored in a government warehouse awaiting payment of duty on re-export.

Under Developed Countries. A term which is being used for developing countries. This term is now used infrequently, in favour of less perjorative terms.

Underemployed Workers. The underemployed worker is one whose marginal rate of substitution of income for leisure is less.

Undervalued Currency. Refers to a currency which, due generally to a balance of payments surplus has been below its free market equilibrium level.

Underwriter. One who agrees to bear a risk, or some part of it, in return for a payment known as an insurance premium.

Underwriting Commission. A commission paid by a company to any person or persons (usually an Issuing House or other financial institution) who guarantees, for the sake of a commission, to take up any shares or debentures offered by the company to the public for which the latter do not subscribe.

Undischarged Bankrupt. Refers to a bankrupt who has not received from the court a certificate of discharge whereby normal business and personal rights are restored.

Undistributed Profits. Refer to profits which are not distributed to shareholders as dividends but which are retained by the company as reserves.

Undistributable Reserves. Refers to the sum of the share premium account; the capital redemption reserve; the amount by which the company's accumulated, unrealized profits, so far as not previously capitalized (except by transfer to a capital redemption reserve), exceed its accumulated, unrealized losses, so far as not previously written off in a reduction of capital; and any other reserves that a company is prohibited from distributing.

Unearned Income. Any type of non-wage income which could be in the form of profits, interest on rent.

Unearned Increment. Refers to an increase in the value of property, etc., which is not brought about by any action on the part of its owner. One example is the increase in market values of all surrounding property which results from the development of a particular property.

Unemployment Benefit. In many countries, it refers to a payment which is made to an individual who is unemployed.

Unemployment Rate. Refers to the number of persons who are capable of working and willing to work but unable to find suitable employment. It is expressed as a percentage of the total number of persons available for employment at any time.

Unequal Exchange. In its strict Marxian form it refers to the exchange of the products of developed economies at prices above their labour values for the products of less developed economies at prices below their labour values.

Unfranked Investment Income. Investment income which is received net of tax, where tax has been deducted at source by the payer, and which is chargeable to corporation tax.

Unfunded Debt. Marketable government securities and treasury bills which have definite redemption dates.

Uniform Costing. The costing systems with a common set of principles and practices operated by different branches of a business or by different undertakings within an industry.

Uniformity. Refers to a situation in which accounting conventions and financial statements are the same for all accounting entities. Uniformity can be more or less rigid depending on the degree to which different accounting treatments are allowed for what are, or are claimed to be different circumstances.

Unintended Inventory Disinvestment. Means rundown of stocks due to an unexpected rise in sales or fall in production.

Unintended Inventory Investment. The term used for the Stocks resulting from the failure of expected orders to materialize.

Union Security. Collective bargaining issues, like check-off and closed-shop, in which the employer helps the union organize and maintain the workforce.

Union Shop. The term used for an arrangement whereby a worker must join the union within a specified period of time after beginning employment. The employer thus has complete discretion in his choice of labour.

Uniqueness. When used in the context of general equilibrium theory it refers to the existence of a unique set of market clearing prices.

Unissued Capital. Capital in the form of shares which a company is authorized to issue but which it has not done so.

Unissued Capital Stock. Refers to the part of the capital stock that has been authorised for issue but has not in fact been issued.

Unissued Share Capital. The difference between the nominal amount of the Authorized Share Capital and the Issued Share Capital.

Unitary Tax. A tax based on a proportion of a business enterprise's worldwide income rather than its income derived in the territory of the fiscal authority.

Unit Cost. In the context of Inventory Valuation, the cost of purchasing or manufacturing identifiable units of inventory (stock).

United Nations Capital Development Fund. A special body which was created by the United Nations General Assembly in 1966 to facilitate economic growth in developing countries by supplementing existing sources of capital assistance with grants and loans.

United Nations Conference on Trade and Development (U.N.C.T.A.D.). An organisation set up by the United Nations to assist the less developed nations, defined as those countries with a gross national product per head of less than $600 a year. It seek to accelerate the growth rate of the less developed countries to not less than 5 per cent per annum. The Conference endeavours to do this by arranging aid and finance, and by promoting trade. In respect of finance, special drawing rights have been made available at the International Monetary Fund to assist the less developed countries when faced with an unexpected slump in their export receipts. The first U.N.C.T.A.D. meeting was held in Chneva in 1964.

United Nations Development Programme (UNDP). The Work

studies in 1961. Already in 1959 the United Nations has created the Special Fund, now the United Nations Development Programme (UNDP) to undertake pre-investment work. It was, and it continues to be, the Bank's policy to refer all requests for financial assistance for sector and feasibility studies to the UNDP.

Unit of Account. The monetary unit in which Accounting Records are kept and in which financial Statements are drawn up.

Unit Tax. A tax based on the weight or size of the Tax Base.

Unit Trust. An undertaking formed to invest in securities (mainly ordinary shares) under the terms of the trust deed. Unlike an Investment Trust it is not a company and is open-ended.

Unit Trust of India. The unit trusts mobilise public savings, by selling their units or ('special' shares) to the public and invest these savings in corporate securities. A unit is simply a pro-rata share in a large but diversified portfolio of corporate securities managed by the trust. A unit trust always stands ready to sell or by back is units at prices based on the current asset value of the units outstanding.

Unlimited Company. A company not having any limit on the liability of its shareholders.

Unlisted Securities. Shares which are not listed on the official Stock Exchange list, but which are traded on the Unlisted Securities Market.

Unquoted Company. Synonym for unlisted company.

Unquoted Investments. Shares and stock of a company not having a stock exchange quotation and which are held by another company. Such investments must be recorded in the holding company's balance sheet at cost or at an estimated current valuation.

Unredeemed Pledge. Refers to an item given as security for a loan which has not been redseemed by repaying the loan.

Unsecured Creditors. Persons to whom debt has been owing, but who have been unconvered or unprotected by prior claims on land, property, and other assets.

Unvalidated Inflation. Means an inflation rate which has been not accompanied by similar rate of increase in the money supply.

Up-market. Refers to that part of a market which caters for the demands of the higher socio-economic groups.

Urban Economics. Means that branch of economics which is able to apply the tools of economic reasoning to the analysis of economic activity in and the economic problems of, cities and towns.

Urbanization Economics. The cost savings which arise when economic activities have been concentrated in urban areas.

User Cost of Capital. The implicit rental value of capital services, or the price a firm should itself pay for the use of the capital stock it owns or is considering acquiring.

Usurious Loans. Loans at exorbitant rates of interest.

Utility. The capacity of a good or service to satisfy a human want. Utility cannot be measured in any definite quantitative form; it is sufficient to be able to say, however, that the utility of commodity A > B > C, and so on.

Utility Function. A function which states that an individual's utility has been dependent upon the goods he consumes and their amounts.

V

Validated Inflation. The inflation which is permitted to persist because the government permits the money supply to expand at the same rate as inflation.

Valuation. (1) Refers to the assessment of value. (2) Also, refers to a quantification in monetary terms of the worth of an item, a group of assets or a business.

Valuation Ratio. The stock-marked valuation of a firm's ordinary shares as a ratio of the book value of assets due to ordinary shareholders.

Valuation Reserves. An amount deducted by a creditor from the book value of debts due to him, in the expectation that some of them are likely to be defaulted.

Value. To an economist this term refers to the 'exchange value' or price of a commodity or service, i.e., the power it possesses of acquiring other goods or services by means of exchange.

Value Added. Refers to the value added to a commodity at each stage of its manufacturer; for example, the value added by a flour miller to the final value of the flour, minus the cost of the wheat.

Value Added Statement. A financial statement disclosing for a period how much value has been added (wealth created) by the operations of an enterprise and how that value has been distributed among employees, government, providers of capital and for reinvestment in the business.

Value Added Tax (VAT). A multi-stage indirect tax. In principle the tax is borne by the final consumer.

Value for Money (VFM) Audit. An examination of the way in which resources are allocated and utilized. Such an audit is concerned with the interrelated concepts of economy (acquiring resources of an appropriate quality for the minimum cost); efficiency (maximizing the amount of output per unit of input); and effectiveness (taking account of the relationship between output and the objectives of an organization).

Value of the Business. A method of Asset Valuation based on the concept that the measure of the value of an asset depend on the loss suffered from being deprived of it. It is also known as value to the owner, value to the firm and deprival value.

Value Theories of. Theories devised to explain the exchange value or price of commodities and services. These have included:

(a) *Labour theory of value:* A theory which states commodities are sold in ratios determined by the amount of labour expended on producing them.

(b) *Cost of production theory of value:* A theory which states that the value of a commodity is governed by the cost of the various factors employed in its production.

(c) *Marginal theory of value:* A theory which states that the value of any commodity or service is determined by its marginal utility for any particular purpose.

Value to the Firm. Synonym for Value To The Business.

Value to the Owner. Synonym for Value To The Business.

Variable Capital. In the Marxian scheme refers to that part of capital, represented by labour power, which undergoes an alternation of value in the production process.

Variable Cost. A cost which, unlike a Fixed Cost, varies, or is assumed to vary, with some measure of capacity (e.g., direct labour hours).

Variable Cost Ratio. The total Variable Costs divided by the total sales.

Variable Proportions, Law of. This law states that if the quantity of one productive service gets increased by equal increments, from zero, the quantities of the other essential productive services remaining fixed, the resulting increments of product will increase for a period, then become constant, and then decrease.

Variable Sampling. In an audit context, sampling plans which are based on quantitative characteristics (monetary amounts) rather than qualitative characteristics. Contrast at Tributes Sampling.

Variance (Accounting). Refers to a deviation of actual results from expected, budgeted or standard results. Variances are usually labelled favourable or unfavourable but should be regarded as attention directors rather than as answers.

Velocity of Circulation. Refers to the average number of times that each unit of money (whether in the form of coins, notes or bank deposits) changes hands in the course of a year. In other words:

$$\text{Average velocity of circualation} = \frac{\text{Volume of spending per year}}{\text{Total volume of money}}$$

Vehicle Currency. In the major foreign exchange trading centres most business is generally carried out in a few major currencies, holders of other currencies converting them into one or other of these major currencies for carrying out their transactions. Such major currencies are called vehicle currencies, and while a number of them are in active use, the US dollor is still the world's principal vehicle currency.

Velocity of Circulation. Means the speed at which a given sum of money circulates in the economy—i.e., the average number of times a unit of money changes hands in a specified time period. One version of the equation of exchange has been as follows:

$$MV=PT$$

where M denotes the money flow, V the velocity of circulation, P the general price level and T the level of transactions.

Vendor's Shares. Refer to the shares in a company which are issued to the seller of a business which is converted into a limited company. The shares are issued as consideration for the sale of the business.

Venture. A business, enterprize or project udertaken, often in association with one or more partners, with a view to making profits, but in which there is a risk of loss.

Venture Capital. Capital for investment in projects which have a high risk potential.

Verbal Agreement. An agreement which has been made verbally (as over the telephone) with no written record.

Verification. An audit procedure (one of the Substantive Tests) the aim of which is to ascertain by the use of appropriate Audit Evidence that assets and liabilities are properly recorded in a balance sheet so far as existence, ownership and valuation are concerned.

Vertical Equity. A tax principle which is supporting the different tax treatment of people in different circumstances.

Vertical Integration. Refers to the amalgamation of firms engaged in the different stages of production of the same commodity to achieve greater economic strength and profitability.

Vertical Merger. Means the amalgamation of two firms who produce products that are belonging belong to different stages of the same production process.

Vertical Phillips Curve. The hypothesis that in the long-run there occurs no trade-off between the rate of money wage change and the level of unemployment as the Phillips curve originally suggested. In contrast to Phillip's original hypothesis, Friedman (1868) has postulated that it is the real wage, not the money wage which is the focus of the wage bargain.

Vertical Supply Curve. Means market situation in which output cannot be permanently expanded by a fiscal or monetary expansion of demand for total output cannot be expanded without improvements in productivity.

Vicious Circles. This term refers to developing countries. This implies that a subsistence economy will remain as such because total output is low, having little or no reserve stocks. Hence, after consumption occurs place there is no surplus for capital accumulation without which there is little hope of increasing output. The key to breaking the vicious circle has been capital accumulation.

Victim Company. A firm which is the subject of a takeover bid.

Vintage Capital Models. These are models of economic growth in with capital is not treated as one homogeneous stock, but as a series of layers of past investment, each layer having its own unique characteristics and representing a more efficient technology than its predecessors.

Vintage Growth Models. Refer to models in economic growth which permit capital and its embodied technical progress to age with time. New innovations only affect new investment, thus the capital stock is composed of differing vintages.

Virement. The use of savings on one subhead of public expenditure to meet overspending on another.

Visible Balance. Means that part of the current of a balance of payments statement, which gives the relationship between the value of physical goods exported and those imported. The other component of the current account has been invisibles e.g., trade in services such as insurance, transport, tourism.

Volume Variances. Variances that arise from deviations from expected, budgeted or standard sales or production volume.

Voluntary-exchange Model. Refers to an approach to the analysis of the provision of public goods which seeks to establish conditions under which these goods can be provided on the basis of unanimous agreement—i.e., without coercion.

Voluntary Liquidation. A situation where the shareholders of a company decide to put the company into liquidation and cease trading.

Voluntary Redundancy. The situation where a worker asks to be made redundant, usually in return for an improved redundancy payment.

Voluntary Winding up. A Winding up in which a company and its creditors are left to settle their affairs without coming to the court.

Voluntary Unemployment. That unemployment which results from the process of job search and speculative and precautionary unemployment.

Votes on Account. The monies granted by Parliament to carry on public services from 1 April of the next financial year until the passing of the Appropriation Act, which authorizes the issue of the amount required for the full year.

Voting Right. The stockholder's right to vote in the affairs of the issuing corporation.

Voting Trust. The transfer by two or more persons of their shares of stock of corporation to a trustee who is to vote the shares and act for such shareholders.

Voucher. A method of provision of some good or service in which individuals have been given funds solely for the purchase of the specified good or service.

Vouching. An audit procedure (one of the Substantive Tests) the aim of which is to ensure that the underlying records accurately reflect the nature of the transactions entered into.

Voyage Account. A profit and loss account not for a period of time but for a particular voyage of a ship.

W

W-2 Form. The annual wage and tax statement all American employers must furnish to their employees, indicating the amounts of Federal income tax, compensation, contributions to social security or other insurance, and state tax (if any) withheld. A copy of this statement must be attached to the employee's Federal and state income tax returns.

Wage. Refers to any regular payment to an employee of a business for his or her labour by the hour, week, month, or some other period, or by units of output.

Wage Audit. A regular review, conducted by consultants, of all forms of payment to employees within a company.

Wage Differentials. The differences in the average levels of pay of groups of workers which are classified according to the industry or location in which they work or according to the occupational or racial group to which they belong.

Wage Drift. The term used for the gap between nationally-negotiated wage-rates and actual earnings which tend to be higher.

Wage Fund. A fund which is available for the payment of wages.

Wage Fund Theory. Adam Smith took over from the physiocrats the idea that wages are advanced to the workers in expectation of the sale of their output. Wages could not be raised unless the capital earmarked to pay them was also raised. Capital, in turn, was determined by savings. The classical school, developed its theory of wages around these ideas.

Wage Indexation. Means the adjustment of wages in line with changes in the cost-of-living. In this way real incomes can be maintained during inflationary periods.

Wage Inflation. Means a rise in money wages over time. It may be due, but need not be, to wage-push inflation.

Wage Leadership. Refers to a characteristic of industries in which productivity has been rising and firms find it easier for a variety of reasons to concede demands for wage increases than to reduce prices.

Wage-price Spiral. Refers to the notion that wage increases cause price increases, via the increase in production costs, which in turn feed through into wages, as workers seek to preserve the purchasing power of their wages, and so on.

Wage-push Inflation. Refers to a variant of cost-push which attributes the origins of the inflationary process to trade union pressure in the labour market.

Wage Rates. The term used for the rate of payment an individual receives for the supply of each of the minimum number of hours specified in the wage contract.

Wages Spiral. Refers to the continuing upward movement in wage levels, occasioned by the attempt through wages increases to offset the effects of inflation on living standards. To the extent that wage increases themselves induce inflation (through price rises needed to cover increased wage costs, or through the expansion of monetary incomes with an upward effect on demand) a continuous interaction between price rises and wage rises results.

Wage Structure. Refers to the ranking of pay levels of different groups of workers classified according to the industry or location in which they work or according to the occupational or racial group to which they belong.

Wagner's Law. A hypothesis, advanced by a German economist Adolph Wagner which stated that the development of an industrialized economy would be accompanied by a rising share of Public Expenditure in Gross National Product.

Walk-through Test. Refers to an auditing procedure in which the processing of typical transactions is followed through all the stages in a client's accounting system.

Wall Street. A street in downtown New York City where a very large percentage of the nation's financial activity is centred. The New York Stock Exchange is on Wall Street and the street is sometimes used as a synonym for that market.

Wall Street. A street in New York where the New York Stock Exchange is located. The term is often used as synonym for the stock exchange.

Walras Law. This law states that given a markets if n-1 markets are in equilibrium then the last one must also be in equilibrium because there cannot be a net excess of demand or supply for goods (including money).

Wanted Capital. The excess of capital stock issued, as its par or stated value, over the fair value of the assets contributed in exchange.

Warrant. Means the buying of an agreement which offers the owner the opportunity to purchase equity capital.

Warranted Rate of Growth. Means the rate of economic growth at which desired saving has been equal to required investment.

Warranty. (1) Express or implied undertakings or declarations made by an insured party to an insurance contract which, it not followed or if incorrect, invalidate the contract. (2) An element or statement of fact contained in a contract which, if broken, does not invalidate the contract. The aggrieved party may, however, claim damages.

Warranty Deed. Also general warranty deed. In real estate law, a document containing certain assurances or guarantees that a Deed conveys a good and unencumbered title.

Warranty Floating. A warranty which may be enforceable by a third party, i.e., by a person not a party to the contract when the warranty is given.

Waste. Material lost in a manufacturing process through evaporation, shrinkage or being left as a residue.

Waste Book. A book in which the entries of transaction are made as they occur. From this book the entries are transferred to other books.

Wasting Asset. Refers to a non-renewable resource such as a copper mine. Extraction or removal results in the physical consumption of the natural resource. A wasting asset may be contrasted with a renewable resource such as a forest where replacement occurs through growth. Wasting assets are said to be subject to depletion rather than depreciation. Their economic life depends upon the speed with which their reserves are extracted.

Watering Assets. Refer to the process of including intangible assets of dubious value in the financial statements of a business, thereby overstating the value of the resources of the business.

Watering Stock. Refers to process of issuing stock of shares in a company either without receiving a corresponding cash inflow or without providing for the maintenance of the previous rates of dividend.

Way-Bill. A document which states a list of goods or passengers carried.

Ways And Means Advances. A method of government borrowing from the Bank of England. It forms only a very small proportion of total government borrowing.

Weakness Letter. A document prepared by auditors setting out shortcomings of systems or deficiencies in financial controls.

Wealth. Goods and other assets in existence at any time which command a market value (i.e., price) if offered for sale.

Wealth, Categories Of. All wealth may be grouped into three categories: (i) Assets that serve as a medium of exchange that is paper money, coins and bank chequing deposits; (ii) Other financial asset, such as bonds earning a fixed rate of interest, that will yield a fixed money value at some future maturity date and that can usually be sold before maturity for a price that fluctuates on the open market. (ii) Claim on real capital that is physical objects and such as factories and machines.

Wealth Effect. Refers to an increase in aggregate expenditure due to a fall in the price level and interest rates.

Wealth Maximization. Refers to the assumption that the objective of a firm (company) is to maximize the wealth of its owners (shareholders).

Wealth Tax. A tax which is levied on net wealth and is normally levied at regular intervals—usually one year—on the net assets of individuals though in some countries such as Norway it is payable by companies as well.

Weightage. The importance to be given to different items included in the calculation of an index number generally indicated as a percentage.

Welfare Economics. A branch of economics which deals with studying the extent to which economic activity maximises human welfare, and the evaluation of public policies relating to the economy designed to achieve that end.

Wholesale. The term used for the intermediate stage in the chain of distribution. Wholesalers specialize in the process of distribution, purchasing the output of firms for re-sale and distribution to retailers.

Wholesale Banking. A term which describes the acceptance of substantial deposits; the provision of loans to business firms and governments; and the earning of profits from dealings in currency and investment transactions. Nearly all banks engage in these activities, but the merchant banks and some overseas banks mainly concern themselves with wholesale banking C.p. Retail Banking.

Wholesale Price Index. An index showing the rises and falls of prices of manufactured goods as they leave the factory.

Wholly-owned Subsidiary. A subsidiary company which is owned 100% by a parent company.

Wicksell Effects. The Wicksell effect shows that contrary to the marginal productivity theory of capital the real rate of interest in the economy may be different from the aggregate marginal product of capital.

Wieser's Law of Costs. A law formulated by Friedrich von Weiser (1851-1926), an Austrian economist. It states that the cost of a commodity is the alternative foregone in producing it.

Wildcat Strike. A strike which is called by local groups of union members, ostensibly without the authorization of the official union leadership and in contravention of established procedures.

Will. A legal declaration of a person's wishes and intentions with reference to the disposal of his or her property after death.

Willingness to Pay. Means the valuation placed by individual on a good or service in terms of money.

Windfall Gains. Profits earned because of some external event rather than by the normal functioning of the business, such as unanticipated Income received from a lottery ticket.

Windfall Losses. Losses arising from actual or prospective receipts which are different from those originally expected and from changes in the net present value of such receipts arising from discount rates different from those originally expected.

Windfall Profit. Refers to any unexpected profit, often unconnected with the normal business of an enterprise.

Windfall Tax. A tax which is levied on a sudden unexpected profit.

Winding up. The process of liquidation of a company. The winding up may be by the court, voluntary, or subject to the supervision of the court.

Winding Dressing. Transactions the substance of which is primarily to alter the appearance of a company's financial statements and the financial ratios derived therefrom.

Windows. Opportunities for profitable investment in markets or transfers between markets; for raising capital in different markets; or for profitable arbitrage taking advantage of fluctuations in interest rates and exchange rates.

Withdrawals (also known as leakages). Any income which is not based on in the circular flow of income, and therefore has been not available for spending on currently produced goods and services.

Withholding Tax. Generally a tax which is levied on dividends and interest made by a company to an overseas destination. Most Western countries have such a tax.

With Profits Policy. A type of life assurance policy in which, in return for higher premiums than on an ordinary life policy, a bonus is paid, being a share of the surplus in the life fund on its revaluations.

Worker Director. A worker who is appointed to the board of a company to represent the workforce.

Working Capital. Capital with which a business works. It is that part of total capital which is used for meeting routine and repetitive expenses of day-to-day business operations, e.g. Working Capital will stand invested in raw materials, stocks, debters, cash and bank balance. Expenses like wages, salaries, rent, rates, etc. are met from these sources. The size of working capital changes every now and then.

Working Capital Ratio. This is calculated by dividing current liabilities into current assets. It has been a measure of a firm's liquidity.

Working Control. The control over a corporation or company comprises, theoretically, ownership of at least 51 per cent of the total voting shares; however, effective control can sometimes be exercised through ownership, individually or by a group acting in concert, of less than 50 per cent of the shares.

Work in Progress Control Account. An account recording in total the direct materials, direct labour and factory overhead charged in detail to individual jobs and recorded in a Subsidary Ledger.

Worksheet. A sheet of calculations in columnar form, used, for example, as an aid to the construction of a consolidated balance sheet or a funds statement.

Work to Rule. A partial form of strike, which results in a slowdown of production rather than complete cessation. Workers insist on producing only according to the strict rules of some written job description or departmental rule and can usually manage seriously to impair productive efficiency.

World Bank. A bank established by signatories to the Bretton Woods Agreement, 1945, in order to make long-term loans to governments to finance postwar reconstruction and to finance development expenditure in less advanced countries. The Bank is backed by share capital subscriptions from member countries and by bonds issued in the money markets. In addition to government lending, the Bank makes loans to private undertakings and provides technical services to governments.

Write Off. (1) The removal of an item from the bookkeeping records at the end of the life of an asset. (2) The transfer of an expense to the profit and loss account statement. (3) To regard a debt as irrecoverable.

Writing-down Allowance. The annual Capital Allowances on plant and machinery and industrial buildings.

Written-down Value. The net amount after depreciation of a fixed asset in the books of an enterprise. Alternatively, the value of the asset for tax purposes after deduction of Capital Allowances. Writtendown values are not designed to be equal to Net Realizable Values and seldom are.

X

X. cp. Abbreviation of ex-capitalisation.

X. d. Abbreviation of ex-dividend.

X-efficiency. A situation in which a firm's total costs are not minimized because the actual output from given inputs is less than the maximum feasible level. This outcome is also termed a situation of 'technical inefficiency.

XD OR X/D. The abbreviation for ex-dividend.

XD OR EX-Dividend. A situation where price quoted for a share in the Stock Exchange does not entitle the purchaser to an ensuing dividend.

XR OR XR, OR EX-Right. Refers to a method of quoting shares in a Stock Exchange, whereby the current purchaser is not entitled to a right of issue by the company which is contemplated or announced to be issued.

Y

Yankee Bond. A bond in dollars issued in the United States by a foreign company.

Yankes. A Stock Exchange term used to describe US securities.

Year-end Adjustment. Where indicated a review and modification of ledger account at the close of a fiscal year.

Year-end Dividend. Refers to an Extra Dividend paid at the end of the fiscal year. Some companies pay such dividends only rarely, after an exceptionally profitable year; other to do so regularly, paying deliberately small regular dividends in order to allow for a year-end dividend.

Year of Assessment. Refers to a period of 12 months commencing on 1st April on one calendar year and ending on 31st March the next calendar year over which an individual's income is measured in order to calculate income tax. (Also known as a 'fiscal year'.)

Year's Purchase. Refers to the value of property is frequently indicated as being equal to the rent for a certain number of year.

Yen. The currency unit of Japan divided into 100 sen.

Yield. A rate of return relating cash invested to cash received (or expected to be received).

Yield Gap. The difference between an average yield on equities and a corresponding yield on long-dated fixed-interest securities.

Yield to Maturity. A Redemption Yield.

Yield Variance. In standard costing, and particularly in process industries the calculation of the actual amounts produced compared with norms or standards and expressing this variance as a percentage.

Yuan. Also known as renminbi. It is the monetary unit of China. It is subdivided into 10 Chiao, the chiao being again subdivided into 10 fen.

Z

Z-chart. A chart which relates to the output of a firm.

Zero Base Budgeting (ZBB). Refers to an approach to the formulation of budgets in which managers have to justify their activities as though those activities were being started for the first time. Analysis and justification is thus shifted away from increments to existing activities and towards a systematic consideration of how objectives should be accomplished.

Zero Net Aid. If the air received in a year from all foreign sources is just equal to the repayment of debt in that year, a country is said to have reached the state of zero net aid.

Zloty. It is the standard currency unit of Poland. It is divided into 100 grosze.

Zone. Trading area, or area to which product launch is temporarily limited a zoned compaign or one that is zonal.

Z-score. Refers to a measure of the solvency of a company, calculated from a linear equation, incorporating more than one financial ratio. The financial ratios used measure attributes such as profitability, working capital, financial risk and liquidity. Neither the ratios nor their weightings are constant over time or space. They are derived by the discriminant analysis of the published financial statements of companies that in the past have failed as against those that have not failed. Z-scores are thus in principle descriptive rather than predictive but they have been successfully used for prediction. Z-scores are measured on an ordinal scale (i.e., one can state that one company's Z-score is greater than another company's but not, say, that it is twice as great) but can be transformed to a ratio scale. This makes possible the calculation of industry-average

Z-scores with which that of a particular company can be compared.

ZPG. Abbreviation of zero population growth. It is an American term for a rate of growth giving a stable population.

Z-score. A measure of the Solvency of a company, calculated from a linear equation, incorporating more than one Financial Ratio.